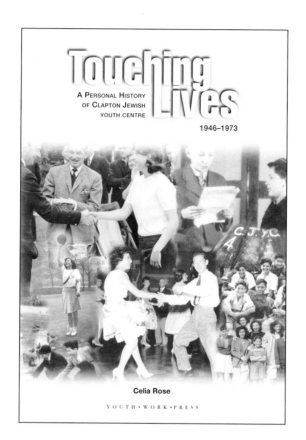

Touching Lives

A PERSONAL HISTORY
OF CLAPTON JEWISH
YOUTH CENTRE

1946–1973

Celia Rose

YOUTH•WORK•PRESS

YOUTH • WORK • PRESS

Printed and published by

17–23 Albion Street, Leicester LE1 6GD.
Tel: 0116.285.6789.
Fax: 0116.247.1043.
E-Mail: nya@nya.org.uk
Internet: http//www.nya.org.uk

ISBN 0 86155 188 5

© April 1998

£8.50

Y O U T H • W O R K • P R E S S
is a publishing imprint of the National Youth Agency

CONTENTS

PREFACE

I have compiled the material for this book from scrapbooks kept while the club was running, from my own personal recollections and from the recollections and views of former members, managers and parents which were gathered through interviews and written replies to a questionnaire.

Some years after the club closed, I thought I would find records to help me with my research. However, nothing had been kept. My sources for the research have therefore centred particularly around the members with whom we have kept in contact over the years. I would like to express my sincere thanks to the 26 people who gave up their time for the interviews and the eight contributors who wrote such detailed reminiscences of their club years. Although I have tried to check all my material as carefully as possible, I would like to apologise to them and anyone associated with the club for any dates or facts which might be incorrect.

I would also like to pay tribute to the Parents' Association who contributed so much financially and socially to the club over the years. My thanks also go to Bill Faulkner for suggesting I write this book and to my family for their encouragement and support.

I have found writing this book a nostalgic and exciting experience. Youth work is not a one-way process. My husband Lou and I would like to thank all the young people we met for the pleasure which our contact with them gave us and as a result the lifelong friendships which we still enjoy.

Celia Rose

INTRODUCTION

Celia Rose has done us a great favour in putting together this book. At one level we can read the words of those involved with Clapton Jewish Youth Centre and gain a vivid picture of what it was like to be there. Perhaps we can connect the experiences and events described with parts of our own lives. However, this book provides us with something more. It highlights some important qualities that have, too often, been forgotten, and it brings out what the long-term impact of youth work might be. It is also an important historical record in its own right.

Over the years young people and workers within the different Jewish youth work traditions have made a fundamental contribution to the development of youth work. From the progressive wing, Lily Montagu worked hard for the advancement and happiness of young women. She was central to the founding of what we now know as Youth Clubs UK, and to developing work in central London for over half a century (through the West Central Girls Club and Settlement). From a more traditional position Basil Henriques was a key figure in the development of boys club work – writing one of the classic texts *Club Leadership*, and cultivating a range of activity for boys and young men through the Bernhard Baron Settlement. Later, workers and trainers such as Sidney Bunt and Sidney Drage (who also both appear in these pages) continued to work for change. The particular virtue of this book is that we can see how such concerns actually worked themselves out in practice. We can also see something of what has been lost in recent years.

While some of the activities and structures described here may seem a little quaint and a product of their time, there is much to be learnt, or re-learnt, from Celia Rose's account. There was something special about work of this kind – and it goes well beyond the particular time and place with which she is concerned. Here I want to focus on four qualities – friendship, participation, religious observance and activity – and how these combine in a concern for association.

One of the things that can be heard in the various voices that make this book is the significant role the club and workers had in promoting friendship. A similar thing can be found in Sorin's account of the Brownsville Jewish Boys' Club in New York. At a time when many workers and policy makers seem to want to justify youth work through the spurious accreditation of the various competencies displayed by young people it is refreshing to read of an approach based on enthusiasm and relationship. Celia and Lou Rose got into the work with no preconceived ideas, but rather acted out of the interests they had. They were concerned with friendship and companionship – of looking to be with young people in ways that allowed them to deepen their appreciation of the commitments, joys and pains of friendship. This links to what one club member describes as the fundamentals of Judaism – tolerance, humility and mercy. In a very real sense, youth work can be justified on these grounds alone.

Second, one of the continuing hallmarks of Jewish youth work is the emphasis on participation – on young people taking on a major role in the organisation and management of both the club and its activities. It could be argued that this was, in part, a reflection of the times, but there is something more here. Alongside friendship there is an interest in mutuality, in using our own resources to make things happen. However, these things happen within a context and we can see some of the tensions around working with a members committee in a structure (the shul) that has other concerns.

Third, there is an interest in the 'Jewishness' of young people. This is, I suppose, to be expected in such an organisation, but within this tradition of work there has been a concern with context – what it means to be Jewish in the everyday situations young people experience. Ralph Goldstaub highlights this here when he talks of the club as a bridge between educational experience and orthodox Jewish background. This can deteriorate into a focus on institutions and symbols but through these pages we can glimpse something more – an open minded engagement with young people's experience.

Fourth, activities – sporting, cultural and social form an important element of the club's success. The workers had their enthusiasms (as did the members) and they were not afraid to share them and to use them as vehicles for the work. I want to stress the 'vehicle' here. While the activities were important in themselves, they were part of something bigger. It was important for members to feel they had done their best, that they had done well, but for the most part this appears to have been linked to a desire to work for the all-round development of members.

These various elements come together in the idea of the 'club'. People come together in association to organise things for their mutual benefit. In youth work 'club' has tended to become associated with 'building'. In recent years with the decline of the municipal youth centre and moves into more short-term pieces of work, the notion of club has been rather pushed onto the sidelines. However, it remains a powerful organising idea. The commitments it embodies, the sense of belonging it brings – and the relationships it fosters – are central to informal education. As Josephine Macalister Brew once argued – a club is a community in the process of educating itself. And this is the predominant feeling that I got from reading Celia Rose's reflections on Clapton. Her book deserves to be read not just in some historical or nostalgic sense, but for what it can tell us about the direction youth work should be taking now.

Mark K. Smith

REFERENCES

Bunt, S. (1975) *Jewish Youth Work in Britain. Past, present and future,*
    London: Bedford Square Press.
Henriques, B. L. Q. (1933) *Club Leadership,*
    Oxford: Oxford University Press.
Montagu, L. (1954) *My Club and I,*
    London: Neville Spearman and Herbert Joseph.
Sorin, G. (1990) *The Nurturing Neighbourhood. Jewish community and the Brownsville Boys' Club 1940–1990,*
    New York: New York University Press.

PART ONE

STARTING THE CLUB

• *Clapton Synagogue with the old club building on the far left.*

**I remember the initial meeting in 1946 in the Shul (to) put
forward the idea of starting the club. The early impressions
were the awful dilapidated building, the marvellous spirit,
the 3d a week sub, the early activities of billiards, table
tennis, board games (and) each club evening ending
with a prayer.**

Letter from male club member, 1946–52

BEGINNINGS

JUST AN IDEA

In December 1945, we returned to London – I with our young children from evacuation in Bedford and my husband Lou from North Africa where he had served with the Eighth Army. Before the war, we had both belonged to sports clubs. Lou was skilled in football and tennis and had been responsible for organising football for his army unit in the desert. My hobby was swimming and I had also worked voluntarily with the Girls Life Brigade in Hoxton, East London. In Bedford, while Lou was away, I was on a committee which arranged hospitality and entertainment for the forces stationed in the area.

For both of us, arranging creative activities for other people gave us personal satisfaction. We didn't really have any preconceived ideas about the needs of young people, or about the aims of a youth club. We were acting out of the interests which we ourselves had. When Lou came home, we felt we would like to put our experiences together and do something worthwhile. We had heard about the successful Jewish youth clubs in East London and, with the large Jewish population now living in Clapton, we felt there could be a need for a club.

GETTING ADVICE

As we had no experience of running a club or indeed of how to go about starting one, we contacted Miriam Moses, one of the pioneers of Jewish youth work. In 1925, she and Elsie Janner, together with three other women, had formed a girls' club at Buxton Street School in the East End of London where Miss Moses was a care worker. In those days it was usual for men and women from the more affluent districts to come to the East End to do voluntary work with underprivileged young people. In 1932 she was Mayor of Stepney and by 1935 the Brady Girls' Club and Settlement had been established, opened by the Duchess of York, now the Queen Mother. Miriam Moses remained its resident warden for 28 years.

• *Miss Miriam Moses, a pioneer of Jewish youth work, pictured with Eamon Andrews in* This is Your Life.

The club stayed open right through the war years and continued to provide not only the usual services for the young people, but also (at the request of the government) hostel facilities, an air raid warden's post and a communal shelter. In March 1945, Miss Moses led a rescue team when the last bomb to fall on London, a V2, almost demolished the Hughes Mansions flats opposite the club, killing 130 people. Still leader of the Brady Girls' Club, she was awarded the OBE for her courage.

She invited Lou and I to the Brady Girls' Club, listened to our proposed project and agreed it would serve a need in the area. She showed us round, telling us how she worked and organised the various activities. She advised us on how to go about starting a club – committees, activities, people to contact – and generally helped us to plan the way for our Clapton club. Through the years she was always available for advice.

STARTING THE CLAPTON JEWISH YOUTH CENTRE

As we were members of the Clapton Synagogue in Lea Bridge Road this seemed the ideal place to start. With the cooperation of the synagogue, a meeting was arranged in March 1946 and eight boys and four girls aged 12 to 13, recruited from the synagogue's religious classes, attended with their parents and five adults from the synagogue. These were children from local grammar schools: Laura Place, Skinners, Hackney Downs, Central Foundation.

Lou asked if they would be interested in forming a youth club, putting an emphasis on sport. The suggestion immediately brought a positive response. It was agreed that we should start to meet in the old house in the synagogue grounds, with Lou taking outside sports activities, particularly football.

However, as Lou was also concerned to get girls' activities going, I concentrated on netball and (mixed) swimming. A meeting of the parents present was also immediately arranged. It was taken for granted that the club would be called Clapton Jewish Youth Centre.

A grandparent of one of the young people, Abraham Leifer, gave a donation of £5 to start the club. With parents of the founder members and representatives of the synagogue, we formed a committee and embarked on a programme. Lou felt that, to get young

• *Abraham Leifer, pictured left with Lou Rose, helped to start the club.*

people interested, there was only one way – through sport. He soon arranged a full sporting programme – football, netball, cricket, athletics, swimming. Within a very short time members were enthusiastically taking part both within the club and with other clubs.

Lou, himself a fine sportsman, always believed that it was important to take part in the true spirit of sportsmanship. According to a tribute in the '50s to Ernest Joseph, well known for his work for the Association for Jewish Youth and the Jewish Lads' Brigade:

> **The sports field is an invaluable, indeed an essential medium for training boys' characters.**

Without spelling it out, this was what Lou was aiming to achieve – for girls as well as boys.

Though Lou introduced sport in the first instance to promote enthusiasm, he was also equally keen to develop a wider programme and encourage members to take part in all the other activities. The communication he enjoyed with the members showed in their participation in this early development of the club.

Indeed, the news soon spread through the schools and, with publicity in the local press, the initial eight boys and four girls had, by May 1946, become 60 members and by July 100 – and still growing.

> **... we have created an atmosphere of friendship and companionship (of) which we feel justly proud.**
> *Club magazine editorial, April 1948*

CLAPTON'S JEWISH COMMUNITY

THE JEWS OF LONDON

The members of the Clapton Jewish Youth Centre were the grandchildren of immigrants who had come to England at the turn of the century, mostly from Russia and Poland. They landed in the dockland area and settled in the East End of London. Though they were uneducated they had skills. They worked mainly in tailoring and dressmaking, often in sweatshops in the houses, and in cabinet making and market trading. They lived in poor conditions in tenement blocks of flats and on council estates, with families sharing old houses and sometimes even rooms.

In 1930 the Jewish population of the East End was over a hundred thousand. (Excluding Hackney, in 1996 it was under six thousand.) However, in the aftermath of the First World War, as the children of the immigrants married, there was a significant northwards movement of Jews from the overcrowded tenements of London's East End. These were the parents of the club members. They moved further afield to Bethnal Green, Hackney, Clapton and Stoke Newington.

Here, though conditions were somewhat better, they still lived in large council blocks of flats and in the shared terraced houses, for example, of north Hackney. They continued in the same trades, with many of them opening small shops and stalls in the markets. Later they went into other trades including hairdressing and home dressmaking, while many of the men trained as taxi drivers. As it was traditionally accepted that the men were the bread-winners, it was unusual for mothers to go out to work.

JEWISH CLAPTON

By the time the club started in 1946, Clapton had a large population of working-class Jews and the Clapton Synagogue flourished. It had a membership of over fourteen hundred families, and there was a large attendance at the cheder, the religious classes.

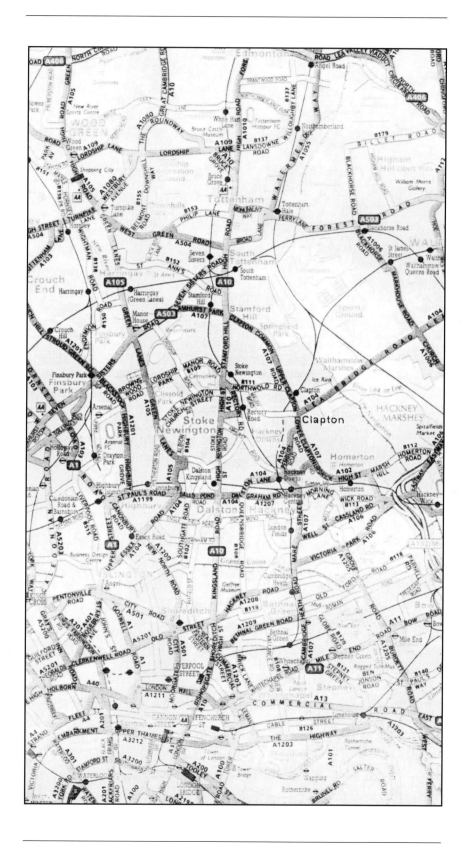

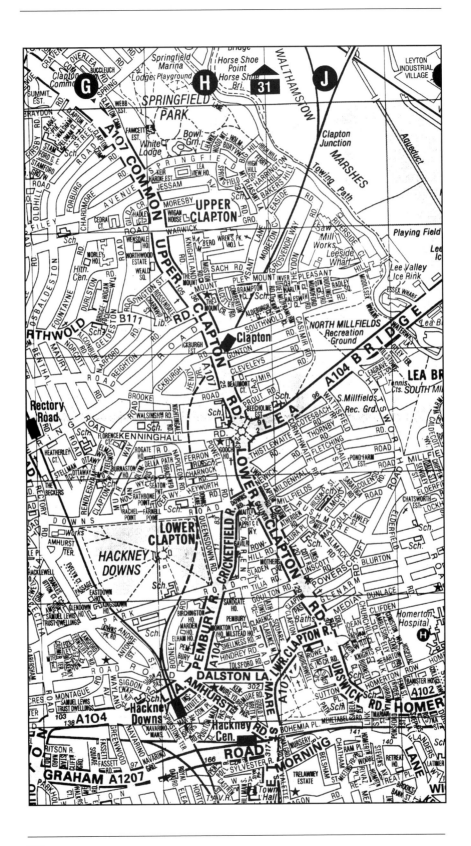

> **... the future of the Clapton Jewish Youth Centre can be regarded as a challenge to the orthodox community of North East London.**
> *AJY magazine* Jewish Youth, *no 12, 1952*

In the '60s the children's attendance at these classes began to decrease. This was partly because many of them were by then attending the large comprehensive Jewish Free School in Camden Town as well as other Jewish schools where religious instruction was given. They therefore only went to the synagogue classes on Sunday morning. From 1965 the club's Sabbath and High Holy Days Children's Services which had been held in the school were held in the club itself (see page 68) as there were no longer the large numbers attending the services.

However, by the early '60s Jewish people were also beginning to move out of Clapton. Young couples in their early 30s, many of whom started married life in council flats or flats in houses, were buying inexpensive houses (for about £2,500) in areas such as Enfield, Chingford, Southgate and Ilford. Their parents often followed them, buying homes near them. Later there was a move further out still, to areas in the north west of outer London such as Stanmore, Edgeware and Finchley, and further north east to parts of Essex. The area of the club was changing. In 1955 the first black people arrived and by 1967 there were many in the area employed as nurses and hospital workers.

From the early '60s the synagogue membership started to fall – a decline which continued steadily over the years. In 1969 when the synagogue celebrated its Golden Jubilee, while many people were there for the occasion, only a very small number were still living in the district. By 1996, though 300 people were still affiliated to the synagogue, most of those still resident in Clapton were elderly. With no new Jewish families moving into the district, from the middle to late '60s the club membership also began to decline.

ANTI-SEMITISM

As a Jewish club meeting on synagogue premises we were allowed to have an all-Jewish membership. If a member brought a non-Jewish friend they were made welcome. However, this rarely happened as Jewish children did not expect to go to a church club and children of other religions did not expect to join a Jewish club.

After the war there was a great deal of neo Nazi activity going on in Hackney with Oswald Mosley and his black shirt followers. One member recalls that when the club was meeting at Detmold Road School there would be groups of non-Jewish boys waiting for them in the street on the way home. Though they taunted them, nothing serious happened.

I remember leaving Detmold Road once. One of the kids had gone down the road and come back and said that there was a gang waiting for us to come out ... there were some boys ready to beat us up. Just as we got down to give the best of ourselves the police came in cars from round the corner.
Interview with male club member/manager, 1949–57

However, the seriousness of the problem was brought home to the club after a very serious incident in 1949 involving two of the members. It is documented in Morris Beckman's book *The 43 Group* (published in 1992 by Centreprise Publications) which describes how a group of Jewish ex-servicemen and women fought in the streets of London to destroy Mosley and his fascists.

One Saturday night, Henry Freedman and Raymond Keene (club members between 1946 and 1954), walking home from their boys' club, had to pass Ridley Road where the fascists were keeping an all-night guard on their pitch for the Sunday meeting. A large crowd, seeing the boys, called after them, 'Dirty little Jew bastards!' This the lads ignored, continuing towards Colverston Crescent where Keene lived. Soon they realised they were being followed by two men. They ran, outstripping their pursuers, but as they reached Keene's house a saloon car came from the other direction.

Keene had no key and, unfortunately, the house was empty. Two men leaped from the car's running board and four more piled out from its interior. All carried bottles or chair legs. The six men rushed up the steps, pinned the boys against the door, and commenced their savage assault. Both boys suffered broken skulls, fractures and internal injuries. They suffered severe facial damage; one had his nose completely smashed. Half an hour after this incident a man passing Ridley Road was attacked and beaten up by the fascists.

Following this, at the request of the Clapton club, a meeting was convened with representatives of the club, the AJY, the Stamford Hill Youth Club and the police. Also present was Sir Basil Henriques who came from a long established Anglo-Jewish family. He had started the Oxford and St George's Boys Club in East London in 1914 which had developed by 1930 into the large and prestigious Bernhard Baron St George's Jewish Settlement. With his wife, he continued as its warden for the rest of his life as well as becoming chairman of the East London Juvenile Court and vice-president of the National Association of Boys' Clubs.

At the meeting the police said that the attack on the two Clapton members was not racial – that it could have happened to anyone. Basil Henriques supported this, claiming the people who carried it out were just vandals. Together he and the police tried to smooth things over by denying that anti-semitism was involved.

However, the Clapton club youth leader at the time, Ralph Goldstaub, took very strong exception to this. As he had come to England from Germany with his family in the 1930s to escape the Nazi persecutions, he was particularly sensitive to the situation. He said that we could not disguise our physical appearance, whatever we might call ourselves, commenting that 'we might call ourselves Clapton and St Mary's but we can't hide the shape of our noses'. The meeting left some bad feelings and brought no satisfaction to the club or its members. Nor did it do anything to help the situation, only making clear that the climate at that time was dangerous and showing up the need to be more vigilant.

MEMBERS AND THEIR BACKGROUNDS

I was 11 years old when I told a bit of a fib because I so wanted to join the club and you couldn't really join until you were 13. But as I was quite tall everybody thought I was much older so I got in.
Interview with female club member, 1946–52

EDUCATION AND JOBS

I was the only working person in the club – I was 14. I left school when I was 13 and started work ... I was not allowed to leave school.
Interview with male club member, 1946–55

In 1947 the school leaving age was raised from 14 to 15, and in 1972 to 16. The girls were not expected to study, just to work for a while and then 'make a good marriage'. A few of them at grammar schools stayed on at school until they were 18 but most left at 15 with no qualifications. A number went to Pitman's (a secretarial college) and others to Miss Goschalk (a private school) to learn shorthand and typing and then into secretarial jobs. Some got taken on as apprentices in dressmaking and hairdressing. They did not seem to have any problems in getting jobs or apprenticeships.

Many of the boys were encouraged to be more ambitious. A good proportion of them in the early years went on to further education at the age of 18 when most then did their National Service. As well as those who went to university, some left school at 16 with matriculation exception and studied optics at a polytechnic. Others were articled to an accountancy or a law firm for five years, studied part-time and took qualifying examinations. There were by then no charges for this. The parents encouraged the boys and later these young professionals often helped their parents financially.

We had a marvellous group of seniors (16+) at that time, very bright kids who had far greater potential than just doing sports and jiving.
Letter from Norman Spector, manager, 1956–63

The educated ones, the academics, they became accountants, solicitors and so on. There were some very bright fellows – our generation ... at the club have done very well. A lot of the boys who didn't study took short-term jobs, a lot of them did like I did – shop work or warehouse work, a lot just waited around until they were old enough to do the knowledge and went into cabs ... Other boys – there was one section in the club that had money – their parents had their own houses and their own businesses ... and worked with (their) Dad.

Interview with male club member/manager, 1949–57

... the groups as they became older did actually separate during the Clapton years in their social lives and went to different places and didn't mix very often. I don't think they liked a few of us who were endowed with a bit of brains and ... seemed to have different hobbies.

Interview with male club member/manager, 1946–52

DRESS, LEISURE AND SOCIAL LIFE

... we didn't have the material things thrust on us. We went to school in our school uniforms and we had our few things – our summer outfit, our winter outfit ...

Interview with female club member, 1949–56

... we were all on a par, none of us had any money, we shared whatever we had, we were good friends and there was never any need to go anywhere else because the club was always there ...

Interview with female club member, 1946–52

In the early years the members would come to the club straight from school in their school uniforms with the boys looking very respectable in their school blazers. The girls came to socials and dances in the latest fashions, though of course the dress scene was always changing. By the early '60s they were wearing pretty dresses with very full skirts and lots of petticoats.

... one of the things I remember now to illustrate the vast differences in youth of today – the boys and particularly the girls would go to the club during the week wearing their school uniforms. I can't imagine that happening today.

Interview with male club member, 1946–52

I would never come to the club in my school uniform – that was something to be got rid of. This was the place to parade for us. I remember a prevailing fashion at one point for the girls was box-pleated skirts and a baggy jumper, little Louis heels were all the go – I'm talking about when we were 11 or 12 and we wanted to look grown up. We thought we were very grown up.

Fred Perry shirts were very popular and they are all the go still. It wasn't jeans. It was very smart actually, nobody wore jeans or sneakers. That was a bit looked down upon. On special Sunday social nights it was like, with the fellers, the bum-freezer Italian jackets with the straight trousers with the little split at the bottom and winkle-pickers. When we were old enough to wear spiky heels, it was winkle-pickers – the longer the toe the better and the spikier the heel the better. In fact, there used to be a thing, I don't know if we had it at Clapton but in other places, if you went to a dance they would issue you with these plastic things to put over the heels because they made dents in the dance floor.

We grew out of the box pleats. My favourite thing was to put on a tight skirt just down to the knee – minis didn't come in till much later – and stocking suspenders. If you lost your suspenders you used a sixpence. I have an abiding memory of trying to jive in a tight skirt, not easy!

Interview with female club member, 1956–61

The leisure activities of the members centred mainly around the club – it was the central part of their lives on weekday evenings and either a Saturday or Sunday night social. They would perhaps make a weekly visit to the cinema, usually over the weekend, to the Regent at Stamford Hill or for a special night out to the Finsbury Park Astoria, a very large and beautiful cinema. Long queues meant you had to get there early to be sure of getting in!

We could earn £5–£6 weekly and felt rich. We were enthusiastic about clothes and music. We loved to dance, arranged parties and went in groups to the cinema. Saturday nights at the Regent, the Ritz or the Super were alive with social possibilities.

Letter from female club member/manager, 1953–60

But their leisure opportunities were limited.

• *Ramble with Ralph Goldstaub.*

... we had the opportunity to meet other young people (and) to be led into certain areas of activity that perhaps youngsters don't always have (now). You saw going out for a ramble was a big deal, going on a train journey. Ralph took us to Chigwell or somewhere like that, which was way out (then) – something that would take you about 10 minutes in the car nowadays. That was quite an exciting thing, it was an expedition.

Interview with male and female club members, 1946–52

There would be visits to other club dances and parties in members' houses. In the mid '50s and '60s the West End discos became popular but this was an expense and for financial reasons a large proportion of the members stayed with the local activities.

On another occasion we had an all night party, pretty racey stuff, not like all night parties now. What it meant was that we all went to Yvonne Bentley's house and at one o'clock in the morning the girls all went upstairs and giggled in one room and the boys all stayed downstairs in another room and in the morning we thought we had had a wonderful time.

Interview with male club member, 1950–59

With boys and girls mixing socially and on holiday, many romances started at the club at an early age. They chopped and changed but many of them lasted and resulted in marriage. In 1955 we had our first club weddings – Lorna Green and Ivor Compton, and Monty Rodel and Evelyn Speigleman – all founder members in 1946, to be followed by many more romances and weddings.

ABILITIES AND ASPIRATIONS

The members' expectations for the future were to establish themselves in a better home than their parents and have a better life. However, many of them had to start very modestly in rented accommodation in the area until they saved up enough money to buy a house. This was the generation which moved away from Clapton into Essex and north west London. Many became active members in their new communities, putting to good use the experience they gained at the club.

When I got to Clapton I found that the membership was a very interesting one. Most of the older members went to selective grammar schools on scholarships and were being considerably better educated than I was. I didn't need to share my culture but they did need help in fitting themselves into this new culture ... They were in need of a club to be a bridge between this educational experience they were having and their orthodox Jewish background. Most of them were in Hebrew schools and came from observant homes, and the club from my point of view had to be the bridge ...

Their school sports ... were all of a very high standard but the club, through the AJY and through the outstanding efforts of Lou, were able to bring to their homes and to their lives a use for this level of achievement in sports and athletics up to a point of sending two members to the Maccabiah sports in Israel.

• *Maccabiah sports in Israel where two members of the Clapton Jewish Youth Centre went to represent their country.*

Similarly ... the fact that the London County Council was able to provide professional instructors gave them an opportunity to have a club activity that was commensurate with what they were getting at school. We ... completely overwhelmed some of the other kinds of clubs that had a less educated membership and less developed children with a vision of themselves as competent people.

Interview with Ralph Goldstaub, full-time club leader, 1948–51

Mostly the women worked, very often taking up training when their children went to school. For many, club friends remained good friends throughout their lives and as far as is known the marriages were happy. No doubt there have been some divorces but it doesn't seem to compare with the proportion of unstable marriages today.

FIRST PROGRAMMES

PREMISES

The first thing I really remember is the building – going up those rickety old stairs – (that) broken down old building.
Interview with female club member, 1946–53

(The) building ... was falling to pieces and was held up by bits of string. The dark dingy basement that we started photography off in ...
Interview with male club member, 1946–52

In 1919 a group of orthodox Jews began to meet for prayers in a house in Mount Pleasant Lane, Upper Clapton. The numbers grew and three years later the Federation of Synagogues raised the £1,800 needed to buy 47 Lea Bridge Road – a very old and dilapidated house. It had a large room on the ground floor, four rooms on the first floor and a basement. The ground floor was used for the synagogue and the first floor rooms for religious instruction classes.

It was in these premises that the club started in 1946. The classrooms were used for activities and the basement for billiards where there was a small table (it was here that many former members recall chalking their cues on the ceiling). In the early evening, table tennis was played in the main room where, after the activities had finished, all the members would congregate for a social and prayers.

ACTIVITIES

At a time when few homes had TV and the need to keep people off the streets was great the club followed the right philosophy in providing a warm stimulating environment, fostering team spirit and a sense of pride and encouraging an atmosphere of Judaism without enforcement.
Letter from male club member/manager, 1946–52

The first club subscription was 3d a week and it was a condition of membership that members must attend two activities a week. After the activities the canteen was opened and the club evening ended with assembly, prayers and a social.

> **I well remember that we used to have to go to activities first before we were allowed to have a social later on. In other words you weren't allowed to just come in and play billiards and sit and chat all evening. You had to do something worthy even if it was only going and listening to pop music. It was by and large a very disciplined sort of place and most people were happy to come and pay their 3d to come in or even pay their 6d if they hadn't appeared for a week and pay in arrears.**
> *Interview with male club member, 1950–59*

> **Yes I think the club did have the right philosophy in our day ... the fact that we had to go to cultural classes before we could go and enjoy ourselves dancing was marvellous. I believe in rules and the club had rules when we were there.**
> *Interview with female club member, 1946–52*

The relationship which developed between the leader, members and helpers working so well together created something very special in these early years. This was to set the tone for the development of the club in the coming years.

The first programmes were created mainly around the skills of the parents, friends and older members of the families. They included:
- drama;
- discussion;
- stamp collecting;
- music (including classical music);
- study group on Jewish affairs;
- photography;
- needlework and handicrafts;
- play reading;
- billiards;
- a concert party;
- table tennis;
- chess and draughts;
- art; and
- first aid.

• *LCC junior drama class.*

• *Cookery classes.*

The first aid group was taken by a St Johns Ambulance instructor, Sam Hecker, who continued to take this group for all the years the club existed.

Grand is the Clapton Youth Centre
Riots of fun, education and variety
Our duties, rehearsals Wednesday and Monday
United and friendly on social day Sunday
Photography, most useful in these days of leisure

Art for those who combine beauty with pleasure
Committee hard working, sincere and friendly
Tournaments arranged with any club readily
Interests for all, girls and boys
Versatile committee help to complete all our joys
Inseparable friendship to all is our aim
Tea in the canteen is not always the same
Improving in time with unity and will
Everybody's wishes we hope to fulfil
So we end with good luck to the CJYC
By a female member (aged I4), Clapton club magazine, 1947

Some of the activities are described in detail below.

Photography

The photography group was run in the dark and dingy basement of the original club building which was falling to pieces. It was organised by Stanley Appel who developed negatives for 1d each. At the age of 12, Stanley was one of the club's founder members (he still has his original membership card). After National Service, aged 20, Stanley started work at the BBC, a career which lasted over forty years. He began in the

"THE CLAPTON RALLY"

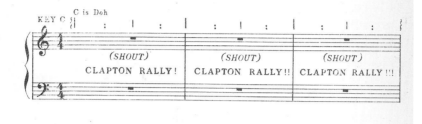

Composed by Mr. and Mrs. Abrahams.
August. 1951.

• *The Clapton Rally*

camera section and eventually become the producer/director (for 25 years) of Top of the Pops and other popular entertainment programmes. He married a club member, Marina Pincus, who joined the club unwillingly – her mother insisted she went, because her brother was a member. Their closest friends today are those they met at the club.

> **I loved the classes ... especially the art, and I loved all the activities: the netball, the swimming galas. I think the rules were right for that time ... I feel that my examples in life were from the club ...**
>
> *Interview with female club member, 1946–52*

The club magazine

At the end of the club's first year, the members produced a magazine, professionally printed, which contained reports of all these activities – for example:

> **CAMERA CLUB**
>
> **Are you a member of the Camera Club. If not, why not? Our meetings are held every Monday in the dark room in the club basement. Why don't you come along next Monday? Who knows, you might be an expert photographer! As you know, the club was formed several weeks ago, and already we have 25 members. We started by doing some printing, and in future weeks we hope to do developing and enlarging. We are fortunate in having Mr Gnessen, one of our parents, who takes a great interest in photography come along to help us. He has given us some interesting talks on the subject, and with his guidance, we hope to make good progress.**
>
> *Club magazine, April 1947*

As well as reports on the activities, the magazines contained articles and letters.

> **(I remember) taking part in reviewing a book ... The Jewish Contribution to Civilisation by Cecil Roth. It gave me ... a feeling that I wanted to pursue more on the subject of Jewish history and I have done that since.**
>
> *Interview with male club member, 1946–52*

As costs became too heavy, after a few years the magazines were duplicated on the gestetner!

• *The first concert party produced by Connie Brill.*

The concert party

The concert party was produced by Connie Brill, a sister of one of the members, who discovered a great deal of talent. It involved about twenty-five members, including several singers, a violinist and actors and actresses. Over a period of 18 months, starting in July 1946, the group gave three concerts at the Dalston County Secondary School, including individual items and short plays.

All the concerts were a sell out, enthusiastically supported by members and parents who filled the large school hall. Local celebrities were also invited. The charge was one shilling, and 3d for members with the profits normally being given to the club. The money for one concert was donated to the British Home for the Deaf and Dumb Women (as it was then known) in Stamford Hill to buy a television. Concerts were also given at Jewish and non-Jewish homes for the aged.

> **Monday, January 26th 1948, found members of the Clapton Club on a unique visit to entertain a party of old folk at the Downs Baptist Mission, at a concert arranged by their secretary, Miss White. A very appreciative audience enjoyed the talents of our members, and we, on our part were highly elated to learn that as a Jewish club we were so well known in the district. We look forward to many more calls on our services to promote goodwill between all faiths.**
>
> **As your concert party and drama class organiser, my special thanks are due to Lorna Greene, Helen Kissin, Sylvia Franklin, Barbara Nathan and Leonard Brill for their very fine performances.**
>
> *Club magazine, April 1948*

Art, music and drama

Though some members opted for Connie Brill's concert party and many others enjoyed the group for pop music, there were some who preferred classical music. A musical appreciation group was formed which, with a manager, played and discussed records and arranged visits to classical concerts.

The art group started slowly but when Mr Roth, a London County Council instructor, was appointed it progressed most successfully and carried on for many years, producing interesting work. A drama group was also started (by Connie Brill) in the very early days of the club.

> **Hackney Dramatic Festival at Dalston County Secondary School First Festival promoted by the Hackney Community League. Play by Clapton – City Frolic. An amusing 'turn' which might well form a diverting feature of a revue but has no particular dramatic claim. Produced by Connie Brill. Adjudicator Harold Warrender, popular broadcaster and actor. Gained third place.**
> Hackney Gazette, *May 1947*

Serving the community: the Norwood Auntie and Uncle scheme

Following contact with the principal of the Norwood Orphanage, Dr Conway, an Auntie and Uncle scheme was introduced into the club. The orphanage, which was situated in East London, was established in 1795. In 1807 the Jews Hospital was opened, catering for small numbers of men, women and children. The numbers grew and in 1861 the foundation stone of a new building was laid in West Norwood to accommodate 220 children. It was called the Jews' Orphan Asylum.

In 1891 the hospital and orphan asylum amalgamated to become known as Norwood. It took children who could not be adequately catered for by parents or relatives, and came to have high esteem in the Jewish community and beyond. After the 1939–45 war it became the Norwood Home for Jewish Children, with the same purpose but also taking some children from local authority homes. In the middle '50s all the children started to move out, to live with foster families and gradually the large building was phased out. In the mid '70s it closed.

The idea of a Norwood Auntie and Uncle scheme came from the Parents' Committee. They were aware that volunteers worked there over the weekends, befriending children and taking them out for the day. They felt that it would be beneficial for children from Norwood to have a day out and come into a home with other young people where there were loving relationships. It was also felt that club members would benefit from befriending the Norwood residents.

Before the scheme started, Dr Conway came to the club to talk about the children and our attitudes towards them. After that, on one Sunday a month for some five years, a party of 25 boys and girls aged between 10 and 13 would arrive at the club from Norwood, to be greeted by club members and parents and spend the day with their families. The visitors were linked up with members of the same age.

The scheme proved a most valuable experience for the club members. For example they discovered that many small things they took for granted were new and exciting to the Norwood children – just being in the kitchen, helping with the chores, even something as simple as making themselves a piece of toast. The scheme was so successful that the Clapton hosts often invited the children for whole weekends and for holidays. Even when the children left Norwood, some of the contacts were maintained.

> **On a visit to Norwood we were shown round by the children and were very shocked to see they slept in dormitories. We had always found it great fun to sleep in a dormitory on club holidays – it was part of the attraction of going – but I don't think it had occurred to us that some children had to do it all the time.**
> *Interview with female club member, 1951–58*

Lou and I had personal experience of this. We were Auntie and Uncle to two children, Rosalind and Brian, who had no family of their own and who were the same age as our children. One incident from 1951 stays in my memory and perhaps captures the experience best. I was combing Rosalind's hair when she said to me: 'Auntie, please do that again, it's wonderful – no-one ever combs my hair.' When we were at Brian's barmitzvah, held at Norwood, and at Rosalind's marriage to a leader from the Habonim Youth Movement at the Habonim David Eder Farm, we were very proud to be introduced as their family.

A youth club library

In 1950, the club was presented with a handsome bookcase to start a club library – one of a number of acts of generosity by Mr Cohen, a parent of one of the members. It was his idea and was well received, especially by the founder members who were by then 16 and 17. Henry Shaw, AJY's religious director, presided over the opening ceremony at which Dr George Webber, president of the Jewish Book Council, gave the key to Maurice Garfield, its first librarian. Through the club experience, Maurice got a job at Shoreditch Library.

This was the first library of Jewish interest to be started in an orthodox Jewish club. Henry Shaw in his speech said: 'In club work, the most difficult task is to foster the educational and cultural aspects of its activities.' He expressed his confidence that the new library would be a wonderful addition to the club.

> **Clapton became Jewish in the accepted historic traditional form and as these aims met local needs they proved successful. The club introduced many innovations in this sphere. To have a library was nothing new, but to make it a library of Jewish interest was a new step.**
> *From the AJY magazine,* Spotlight, *1952*

For several years the library was a success, with parents and friends donating encyclopaedias and books of Jewish interest and on history. It was well organised and the books were in regular circulation. However, even though the membership became larger, in later years interest in it gradually declined. It no longer attracted the changing interests of the members and it was hardly used.

> **I was ... making use of the Club library. I certainly attribute the beginnings of what literary taste I have to the Club.**
> *'What my club meant to me', AJY magazine, 1957, by male club member/manager, 1946–52*

COMPETITIONS

When the club started, competitions were internal and the club committee decided to divide the membership into four houses. Their names, chosen after study and discussion of famous figures from Jewish history, were Wedgewood, Roosevelt, Balfour and Wingate (one of the magazines of the time included a letter from Mrs Lorna Wingate marking Chanukah, the Festival of Lights, when the Jews remember some of their heroes. She was the widow of Orde Wingate, a distinguished general killed in a plane crash in 1944 who, though not a Jew, had been an ardent Zionist and had organised Jewish volunteer forces in Palestine between 1936 and 1938).

We have all worked very well together in all the competitions. We were leading in the house shield until Roosevelt pipped us on the post in the clothing drive. Congratulations to them, but they'd better watch their step – we mean to get there next time.

Wedgewood House Captain, club magazine, April 1947

Within the first year a sports day was held at Victoria Park, Hackney. It produced great support and enthusiasm among members and parents. A cup was donated by the president of the club, Mr Roberts, which was presented to the captain of the winning house.

Other inter-house competitions – for example, table tennis and athletics – were held within the club. Points were given for each competition and at the end of the year the winning house was presented with a merit shield. The reports in the magazines from the house captains reveal a friendly rivalry between the houses.

We have lost the most coveted House Shield, which represents the ability of the house in cultural, indoor games, and sport. I am not going to make excuses or prophecies for the next Shield Competition, but we members of the Wingate House must show more enthusiasm and more of that competitive spirit.

Club magazine, April 1948

In 1946 one of the parents gave money to establish an event in memory of his mother – a prize day to be called The Leah Cohen Prize-giving event. At this, books were presented to outstanding club members and the winners of club competitions for sporting and cultural achievements. The event

• *CJYC sports day – Balfour boys' captain, Malcolm Stella, with house cup.*

was to become a major one in the club year and continued for many years. It was conducted with great ceremony in front of many VIPs which always included the Mayor of Hackney, the Rabbi from the Clapton Synagogue, the local MP, representatives from the national youth organisations and a large gathering of members and parents. It was always a very exciting event.

After the first year, in 1947, as the club began to win cups and medals from the AJY and other national youth club associations, fewer awards were gradually made through the internal competitions. Nonetheless, the display of successes within the club contributed to the excitement and success of the prize-giving event.

> **... from all the AJY clubs provisionally affiliated, we were the only club to receive full affiliation during the past year, and also to have been given full affiliation to the London Federation of Boys' Clubs.**
> *Club leader's report, club magazine, April 1948*

PAID LEADERSHIP

After one year (1947), with the membership at 100 and growing rapidly, the work and time involved were making great demands on the small number of workers, myself and Lou included, who were responsible for the administration of the club. This meant being at the club when it opened (the juniors came at 5pm), preparing for all the activities, arranging the canteen, and then staying until the club closed at 10pm – though the leaders were usually there until about 10.30pm.

The committee, which consisted mainly of parents of members together with representatives of the synagogue, discussed the situation and decided that, provided funds could be found, the club should have a paid leader. With no grants from the local borough in those days, the Parents' Association – which was already holding functions to raise money – agreed to give £200 a year towards this. The synagogue also offered a contribution of £100 a year. The United Synagogue Welfare Committee who were paying for an officiant at the club's sabbath morning childrens' services were also prepared to give the club a grant towards religious education.

These donations enabled the club to employ its first club leader. It was fortunate in finding a very suitable candidate, Henry Koor, an orthodox young man who brought many new ideas and an interesting approach to club work.

PART TWO

THE CLUB AT ITS PEAK

• *Club members on holiday at Bracklesham Bay.*

To rank equally with the oldest and best clubs on the sports field, to occupy a leading position in many activities of the London Federation (of Boys' Clubs) and the London Union (of Youth Clubs) to lead AJY in its intensity of Jewish feeling and enthusiasm, and to accomplish all this in six years is the amazing record of the Clapton Jewish Youth Centre.

From the AJY magazine, Jewish Youth, *no 12, 1952*

KEEPING THE CLUB RUNNING

MAKING DECISIONS AND RAISING MONEY

The club was run by a council, a club committee and a number of subcommittees.

COUNCIL

Chairman Secretary Treasurer Club Leader + representatives of
Managers, Parents, Aid Committee, Synagogue Committee

COUNCIL EXECUTIVE

Chairman   Secretary   Treasurer   Club Leader   Synagogue Representative

Club Committee   Managers' Committee

Sports   Social   Magazine   Central British Fund
Subcommittee   Subcommittee   Subcommittee   Subcommittee

THE CLUB COUNCIL

The Club Council was made up of representatives from all the main sections and groups involved in the club including leaders and managers, the parents and the synagogue. It met regularly with the representatives from the Club Committee to discuss the reports they had prepared. It was responsible for appointing the club leader and approving their salary and expenses and had the overall power to review, criticise and generally supervise the running of the club. The Council Executive, made up of its chairman, secretary and treasurer, the club leader and a synagogue representative, met more frequently to deal with the budget, expenditure and, later, grants from the borough council. It was also responsible for responding to any serious problems which had arisen.

There were occasions when there was some conflict with the synagogue: it did not always approve of the club's procedures or ways of operating which it sometimes felt were too permissive.

> **... many people on the Shul (synagogue) Council were really not the ideal people to be guided into youth clubs**
> *Interview with male club member/manager, 1949–57*

The members also resented members of the synagogue coming into the club to demand that some of the boys leave their activities and go into the evening service to form a minyan (that is, to help make up the 10 adult males required for the service to be held).

> **(When I first joined) I was too young to be roped in for a minyan (for services in the synagogue) so I didn't have to run around the building to hide when they came searching for a minyan ...**
> *Interview with male club member/manager, 1946–52*

However, with tact and goodwill we overcame these problems.

For many years the key positions of responsibility in the club of chairman, secretary and treasurer were held by the people who had originally been connected with the club when it was founded. Over the years others who worked with them did take over including one founder club member, Martin Compton, who eventually became club chairman in 1964.

THE AID COMMITTEE

This was set up by a local business man with about eight other people (business contacts and friends). It had Miriam Moses and David Weizman MP as joint presidents and ran fundraising functions and events often involving club members. These included:
- In 1951, a concert at the Alexandra Theatre, Stoke Newington, compered by Eamon Andrews before he became famous as a television personality.

- In October 1950, also at the Alexandra Theatre, a play, *My One and Only*, performed by the well-known Yiddish Theatre Company which raised £500.
- A garden party held at a beautiful residence in Hampstead in July 1951.

The committee raised a considerable sum of money. Unfortunately, however, the person who had volunteered his services as both treasurer and secretary suddenly emigrated to Australia with the funds he was holding at the time (though he did have wider community connections, he was not a local man!). This rather dampened the other members' enthusiasm and the committee disbanded.

MANAGERS' COMMITTEE

The Managers' Committee was made up of all the voluntary helpers – what the term 'manager' meant in Jewish youth club circles at the time. They were responsible for the programmes and the day-to-day administration of the club and would meet, normally monthly, with the club leader and also have regular meetings with the Club Committee. They also often had extra meetings during club time.

CLUB MEMBERS' COMMITTEE

The only committee which was democratically formed was the Club Members' Committee. The elections, held each year at an AGM run according to all the correct procedures, always attracted many contenders for places on it. Though the committee did not deal with the group programmes, it took responsibility for arranging socials, dances and special club events. It was also free to comment on all aspects of the club and would try to resolve any problems which arose, such as members being disruptive, and when necessary ask the club leader to deal with them. It thus became an important way for members to be involved in decision making and get experience of carrying responsibility. It also had meetings with the Managers' Committee.

... membership of the committee gave me the confidence in speaking out and in learning the procedures of meetings, and

in clear constructive thinking.
Letter from male club member/manager, 1946–60

I think the turning point to my attitude to the club came when I was asked to be on the committee ... Up till then I had the impression that the club ran itself on our subscriptions and that the leaders and managers were only there to turn off the lights when everyone had gone home.
'What my club meant to me', AJY magazine, 1957, by male club member/manager, 1946–52

SUBCOMMITTEES

The club subcommittees, as well as including members of the main committee, involved club members who volunteered because they were interested in a particular group or activity. They too enabled members to gain experience of responsibility.

By the time I was 13 I was busy on every committee I could join ... I learned committee skills which I use to this day ... I began to help with Junior Club on Sunday afternoons, returning in the evenings to help with our Sunday socials ... I was a leader on a Junior Club holiday ... and continued to attend the Club until after my eighteenth birthday ... Club activities gave me confidence and the propensity for assuming responsibility for anything!
Letter from female club member/manager, 1953–60

I am where I am today due entirely to the arena that was allowed me in my early years which gave me the confidence and experience to 'organise'.
Letter from male club member/manager, 1949–57

I am sure the years at the club influenced my life. They gave me a certain confidence ... If I wanted to be on committees or I wanted to do something I knew how to organise.
Interview with male club member/manager, 1946–68

... it's all about organising – it's all about training ... about leadership and encouraging people. The club taught me something in the very early days, when I was 14 or 15 – leadership is about sharing your successes and hiding your fears.
Interview with male club member/manager, 1949–57

I enjoyed being club captain. It did not involve an awful lot of responsibility other than chairing committees and saying a few words at assembly each evening. But I think it stood me in good stead for management responsibilities later on.
Interview with male club member, 1950–59

The committees worked well together most of the time with the club leader being the link. In addition, in the early years, I worked very closely with the first club leaders. Informally I would also meet with them very often to discuss club matters and plan programmes.

THE PARENTS' ASSOCIATION

Even though the Clapton Synagogue and the United Synagogue Welfare Committee had promised grants, the Club Committee's decision in 1947 to employ a full-time leader raised concerns about finance. Would the grants fully cover the costs? Were we over committing ourselves? I consulted with Dr Sidney Gold, then chairman of the Association for Jewish Youth, on how the club could raise money. His advice was: 'Go to your parents – the club is for their children – make money their worry.'

Acting on his advice, a meeting of parents was called at which Dr Gold spoke on the importance of the club. When he suggested forming a Parents' Association, the parents immediately acted on his advice and a committee was formed. The inauguration of the Association in July

• *The Parents' Association.*

1947 was a vital step in the history of the club since it was to play an important role in the development of the club.

From the beginning, it was well organised, with representatives from the club and the synagogue. The parents quickly began to arrange functions and raise money – dances at the Stoke Newington Town Hall at 5s a ticket, regular whist drives in members' houses, a wonderful garden party at a large house in Hampstead, and many other events. In addition there were regular (non-fundraising) meetings with speakers.

Within a year, the Association was contributing a monthly banker's order for £17.50 towards the club leader's salary. It also provided money for equipment – a typewriter, a Gestetner duplicator, a small Ark for the Childrens' Service, indoor games and tools and materials for the handicraft group.

> **It is my opinion that every parent should make some effort, however small, to associate themselves with the club to which their children belong. A successfully run Parents' Association can help enormously in making this possible, and besides gaining the goodwill and help of the parents, such an Association can become a centre of social and cultural activity in the district.**
>
> *By Celia Rose, in the AJY magazine,* Spotlight, *1951*

Some of the parents also became directly involved in the work in the club – for example, by taking group activities and running the canteen. However, because the club became so large members seemed to ignore the presence of some of their parents while others were quite proud of their involvement.

> **Something I think was very positive (was) that there was a Parents' Association. It wasn't just a place for the parents to get rid of their children. The parents were participating and influencing the club ... quite a lot of them were involved. It may have been a bridge between parents and children ... a place where they could meet, a common interest. This is lacking now. Very often parents go one way and children go the other ... I don't know if children would accept parents helping them with their club now.**
>
> *Interview with male and female club members ,1946–52*

The Parents' Association worked independently though with representatives on the club council and with several of them working also as managers. It continued to flourish throughout the life of the club, with parents continuing to stay involved even when their own children left the club. In later years too, new parents took over, even if in a more limited way.

In fact the Association became an important extension of the club, as a cultural and social centre for adults in the community – a club in its own right. Members joined in each others celebrations and gave each other help and support in times of trouble. They met socially, took holidays together – for example, at Bracklesham Bay in the 50s – and arranged outings. (On one of these outings, during a seaside game of cricket when Lou had been batting for a long time, someone called out: 'He's red hot.' And he really was. He'd put his pipe, still alight, into his pocket and it was burning a large hole in his trousers!)

A spirit of friendship developed among those involved in the Association which lasted a lifetime.

> **Although not the first club to organise a Parents' Association there is little doubt that the parents in the (Clapton) district are among the most active in the AJY. In addition to relieving part of the financial burden from the Club committee ... the Association does much in the sphere of adult social life in the locality.**
>
> *From the AJY magazine,* Jewish Youth, *no 12, 1952*

> **We all got friendly together because their children were the same age as ours ... We had days out together, coach outings ... We helped in the canteen – we were very active in the club ... We raised money for the club – we ran dances. We also encouraged the boys to run dances which they did themselves ... and ran them well.**
>
> *Interview with Betty Silver, member of the Parents' Association*

PREMISES

I think I jumped the queue as my recollection is that you had a long waiting list in those days ... The place was always full – there was always a queue outside to come in.
Interview with club member, 1950–59

In this story of success lie the seeds of grave problems and these are now sprouting rapidly and strongly. The club has developed so well, it has so many activities that it has quite inadequate accommodation ...
From the AJY magazine, Jewish Youth, *no 12, 1952*

EXPANSION – DETMOLD ROAD SCHOOL

By 1950 the club's membership had reached the two hundred mark, all over 13, but in 1951 the club opened up a section for 10 to 13-year-olds. Many of the existing members had brothers and sisters who were anxiously waiting for this and there had been many requests for it from parents. Within a few weeks, this was closed with a membership at 70.

The full-time leader at the time, Ralph Goldstaub, concluded that the club had by then outgrown the synagogue premises. He made the radical proposal that some of the activities should be transferred to a local school on Detmold Road. However, as it was about 10 minutes walk from the club building at the end of a long side turning, it was not easily accessible. Would the members be prepared to go?

Ralph, who was always full of optimism and ready to press forward with new ideas, was willing to experiment. He introduced London County Council 'instructors' who, though there were no grants for club leaders, came at no charge to the club. A programme was arranged using the club and the school. The activities at the club were taken by voluntary workers – the helpers we called managers. The school programmes were all taken by the LCC instructors.

The club building was open from 5pm and the school from 7pm until 9.15pm, with everyone back in the club for canteen and social activity

• Table tennis was always a popular choice of activity for members.

until l0.30pm. By staggering the times and the age groups in this way, the club was able to cater for 250 members.

The under 13s met at the club. The activities there still included needlework, fretwork, dramatics, discussion, table tennis and photography. On Sunday afternoons, Hebrew folk dancing and singing and indoor games were organised. At the school, the LCC instructors provided ballroom dancing, drama, handicrafts including ceramics, PT and table tennis coaching. There was also a very full sporting programme for boys and girls in all age groups.

> **... when the club split up into more than one venue I think it lost some of its cohesiveness (though) that's total hindsight.**
> *Interview with male club member, 1946–52*

Once a month a dance was held in the school hall in addition to the socials held at the club every Sunday evening. These dances and socials were run completely by the members. From time to time, on a Saturday or Sunday evening, Ralph would invite interesting people to meet and speak to the members at the school and lay on a 'tea-party'. Despite taking place in the rather bleak hall of the school, he managed to introduce an atmosphere of elegance and high standards which the members loved. (These evenings are described more fully below, see page 53.)

SPRUCING UP THE PREMISES

> **... today you wouldn't be allowed to occupy the old house as a youth club – safety would never allow you to do it. The**

stairs were falling in, the ceiling was falling in as was everything else ...
Interview with male club member/manager, 1949–57

While the club was successful and happy, there was a growing concern about the appearance of the premises. (It hadn't been helped over the years by members screwing holes into the ceiling above the small billiard table to chalk their cues!) One evening when a member of the AJY was visiting the club, a discussion with some of the managers ensued about the dilapidated appearance of the building. The visitor's comment was: 'Why don't you do something about it – you could start with the curtains.'

As for many of the members the club had become a family and this was their 'home', this remark made them feel that they should take more pride in the building. The Club Committee also discussed the situation with the parents. The result was an exciting project. The parents through their committee agreed to pay for and make the curtains. The Club Committee was involved in choosing the material. The members painted the walls and the club was transformed. It made a great difference to the club atmosphere generally as members had not always been too particular about how they treated the premises. When the work was finished, they were more careful about litter, helped to tidy up and took pride in their new-look premises.

A NEW BUILDING

The Clapton Jewish Youth Centre has recently taken occupation of their new club premises, a floor in the new synagogue building erected at Clapton. This club is one of the great success stories in the AJY ... This fine club, with its positive Jewish tradition, (has been) built up within a few years from a small struggling group to one of the largest and most successful in the Jewish Youth movement.
From the AJY magazine, Spotlight, *1954*

When the synagogue decided to build a new community centre, all consideration was given to our needs. The cooperation with the synagogue was largely the result of the efforts of the chairman of the Parents' Association, Morris Leifer, then vice-president of the synagogue who was later to become its president. His father, Abraham Leifer who named the hall, wanted to have pleasure from it while he was alive rather than it just becoming a memorial.

The club was anxious to have space completely independent of the synagogue because, as in other clubs, sharing premises with other organisations within the synagogues had meant problems over storing equipment and setting up noticeboards and often too with caretakers. As a result of meetings between the club council and synagogue officials, the plans allowed for the club to have a floor of its own. The club raised some of the money for this. The Raven family, who were members of the synagogue, named the hall in memory of their brother, Charles Raven, while the Parents' Association paid for the canteen's furnishing and equipment.

The existing synagogue building was demolished in 1953. We were sad to see it go – it had so many happy memories. But everyone involved was happy, to know that it was making way for a brand new building to house the club. During the year of rebuilding, all activities were held in the Detmold Road School premises.

At last, in 1954, the new building was ready. It was opened by Victor Mishcon, at the time chairman of LCC. It was celebrated with a function in the hall which was attended by the Mayor and Mayoress of Hackney, Rabbi Rashbass of the Clapton Synagogue and local dignitaries and representatives of the youth movements. A large gathering of parents and members were also there.

• *1954 – opening of the new premises, pictured left to right: Lou Rose, Celia Rose, Jack Silver, Rose Leifer, Jack Herman, Mrs Rashbass, Rabbi Rashbass, Ethel Herman, Mayor of Hackney, and Mr and Mrs Victor Mishcon.*

It had a large communal hall with kitchens for use by the synagogue and to be hired out for functions and as a banqueting suite. On the first floor, six rooms had been provided for the synagogue education classes. And the top floor was for the youth club's exclusive use – at no charge. This made Clapton the only synagogue club with its own premises actually within synagogue premises at that time.

The club floor consisted of a hall, an office, ample storage space and a canteen with all new kitchen fittings, a serving bar, a long settee, and tables and chairs. The whole floor was beautifully finished with curtains chosen by the club committee, colourful chairs and two desks and fitments in the office.

It was very different because we were in someone else's building. It was an institution whereas in the old building it seemed to be an old building that people just used and enjoyed themselves (in).
Interview with male club member, 1951–59

So, the Clapton Jewish Youth Centre has been opened – the culmination of all the dreams of the children who have grown into young men and women and who have moulded their characters in the club's old building. Oh! the stories that building could have told! All the heartaches, sorrows, joys and happiness of adolescents fast growing up to take their part in the world of trouble and little rest. Here they learnt to take criticism, to share attention, to overcome their shy ways, and in general to mix with other children the same age as they. The ramshackle old house showed on its walls the efforts of the club members to be cartoonists, their opinions of fellow members, (not often complimentary), and the scars of angry fists and feet that beat out their anger against its falling plaster.

How ... gladly those wonderful memories come – of the Junior Club play acted in our ramshackle two rooms, of oratory competitions practised in a classroom up the rickety stairs and of Sunday evening socials in the Intermediate Club (when we of that section, were, of course, the cat's whiskers).

Now, when I go up the flights of stairs into our new fresh club hall, I have a feeling of excitement in me, and my throat is dry because I still cannot believe our good fortune in having such a wonderful place of our own. Our club is a family, generally a happy one, but as with all families we have our ups and downs, our outstanding rebels and our

quiet even-tempered members who cure our hurt pride with the balm of common sense.

I am pleased that we had to start our club life in a slum of a house, yes, pleased – for through that house, whose every nook and cranny we knew, we grew together, our numbers restricted themselves for anyone who had no wish to keep the pace of a growing club also had no wish to stay with Clapton. Yet, our waiting list grew.

The club leaders, I am sure, must have suffered as many heartaches as anyone else with the old house. No room for this activity – no space for that one – no proper canteen – no proper office. But I often dream of our old building, and my dreams are always happy. I dream of warm Summer days and of cold Winter ones, but always I dream of laughter and sunshine in the hearts of the members of a young youth club.

Then down came the bricks, and with every stone and flurry of dust, a memory lay revealed to the public eye. I was unhappy to see our building go but watched with swollen pride our new communal centre rise out of the ground, and when it was finished how we, the now senior and seemingly grown up members of the club, ran over the floors of the club hall, enjoyed its new canteen, exclaimed over its furnishings, and treasured its newness. I look and wonder at the new junior club and watch them take for granted something that we never knew, a safe and beautiful home for our club family. When this building is old, what memories will it hold for them? Or for us?

I pray that those memories may be as full and as beautiful as the ones that lay buried with the debris of the old house.

A member's account, 1954

In addition every evening the club was allowed to use the six classrooms for group activities as the synagogue classes finished early. The communal hall kitchen was also made available for cookery classes while the communal hall itself, as well as being used for indoor games and PT and staging large fundraising shows, was also the venue for dances arranged by members.

With this space available the club continued to grow and develop. When the membership reached 360 a waiting list had to be started. To cope with the large numbers, the programme was arranged so that different age groups met on different evenings and with the juniors having their sessions early before the older members began.

LEADERSHIP

Without the club and without the leadership I think probably my teenage years would have been less than they were. Because having lost my father at the age of 10 I had no other father figure in my life ... On looking back Ralph [the full-time leader] was the father figure for me.
Interview with male club member, 1946–52

I always felt safe when I went to the club and in a secure environment ... It was important how he (Lou) thought of us and many things we might have done I assume we didn't do because we wouldn't have wanted him to be disappointed in us. He was very important. Often when we arrived at the club (he) would give us a cuddle and welcome us in and you never ever felt threatened by that cuddle ...
Interview with female club member, 1962–67

The following are pen pictures of the paid leaders – most of them full-time – who particularly contributed to the development and philosophy of the club throughout its history.

Henry Koor (1947–49)

As we have seen, in 1947 with the club membership at 200 and growing fast, the club council decided that it was too difficult to run the club without a full-time leader to take overall responsibility. They advertised the post and appointed Henry Koor as the club's first full-time club leader.

Henry had no formal training for youth work but was a student of the Yeshiva (an orthodox Jewish school of learning) and experienced in Jewish youth club organisations. In the comparatively short time he was leader (two years) he made a great impact. A very sincere young man, his philosophy was to show young people that they could be intellectual and observant and at the same time enjoy sporting and social activities. He was a good sportsman himself and entered fully into the sports activities with the members.

He was keen, too, on the arts, such as music and drama, and was well informed about them. He introduced some interesting programmes, taking part in many of them himself, particularly discussion groups.

Kind and compassionate, Henry gained the confidence of the members and also of the volunteers who at that time were the parents. He always found time to talk with people and his wise counsel was appreciated. He communicated as well with the girls as the boys, breaking down the barrier between boys' and girls' leadership. Because he was never clinical in his approach, was always there when needed and gave his time unstintingly to the club, he was listened to and respected.

Lou and I worked closely with him, Lou on the sport and I on the programming administration and welfare of the members. To me he was a very special person and a great support. There were often problems, sometimes with members, sometimes clashes of personalities between managers. Henry was always calm, rational and seemed to be able to sympathise with all points of view. On many occasions after a club evening we would often confer on the phone till midnight.

On one occasion, a glorious summer afternoon, Lou was at football and Henry was elsewhere with members. With a manager I was taking a ramble with about twenty juniors. My son Alan, who was then about 9 years old, would not keep up with the group. He was lagging behind and being a nuisance. This aggravated me and was an embarrassment. When I told Henry about it afterwards, his comment had a great impact on me: 'You can hardly blame Alan. It was a hot afternoon and perhaps you should have been in the garden with your children enjoying the fun in a paddling pool. Why should he have to share you with 20 other children?'

Henry married, had a family and eventually emigrated to Israel. Unfortunately he died at an early age.

Ralph Goldstaub (1948–51)

Ralph had an unusual and exciting approach to youth work. He would always dress well and often in those days smoked a cigar. He presented himself with an air of importance which was not always popular with colleagues from other clubs who could think him arrogant. It was certainly not the usual image of the youth club leader at that time – but then Ralph was not the usual club leader.

In an interview for this book, Ralph gave his own account of his experiences of getting into youth work and of becoming the full-time leader at Clapton.

I came to England in 1936. I was 14 and went to a boarding school in Hove for about three years. Then the war broke out

and I volunteered for the Royal Air Force. I was later transferred to intelligence work with my knowledge of German.

When I came out of the Air Force I wanted to go to the London School of Economics to study social work but there was a two year waiting period. I was very unhappy to sit around for two years doing nothing. I had a friend who was a club leader at the Stoke Club for Boys who heard of a new programme in Bristol – a one-year course leading to a certificate in youth leadership. The course ran parallel to the graduate teachers' one-year teaching diploma. I went to a selection weekend and was one of a group of people selected … I then went around the Jewish community trying to get sponsorship to hopefully get some money in promise of a job (after) going to Bristol.

My first visit was to Basil Henriques. I told him how much I admired what he had done for youth work and that I had been accepted for this training course and did he have any suggestions how I could have connection with Jewish community youth work both at school and after. His reply was that the whole idea of youth leadership training was ridiculous, that youth leadership was a way of bringing together young people from universities and public schools who have had all the advantages of a good education and a good home and for them to come and share it with the less fortunate at a kind of settlement house or club. I thanked him.

(I then) had an interview with a leader at Hackney Club who was very interested in my interest in youth work. He said that he felt I had a future in youth work and I could work for him now and learn the business. (As) he would be retiring in a few years and I would inherit the job of club leader, (I should) forget all about professional training. All that needed to be known he could teach me as his assistant. I thanked him and went to Bristol.

I came back and went to the London School of Economics. After a few months I received a letter from the people administrating university grants to servicemen telling me that it was not their policy to pay for two lots of qualifications. I was a qualified youth leader and (so should) forget about going to the London School of Economics for social work training … (and) was approached for the boys' club leadership at Clapton.

From an interview with Ralph Goldstaub, club leader, 1948–51

In his interview, Ralph also reflected on the role of the club at that time and the part it could play in its members' lives.

This is where I as a professional club leader came in, to help these young people who were sometimes a little lost in the world of academics or alternatively were happy in the world of academics and found themselves in difficulty with their families, who perhaps felt slightly snubbed – not many but some.

The reason why the leader was important in their life was because I was this bridge between the two worlds that they were in: the newly opened up world of education and learning and sports achievement and arts and the older world of their parents and Hebrew school and a home which they were attached to. It wasn't that they were rebelling against this. They needed somehow to bring these two experiences together. This is where Clapton was able to help, not just with professional leadership, but with some of the volunteers, the committee, the chairman. We were able to help them fit comfortably into both worlds at the same time.

From an interview with Ralph Goldstaub, club leader, 1948–51

Though Ralph's programme was always carefully planned, whether it was a junior club tour of London or a club holiday, something special and unexpected would be laid on. For example, though today being out at midnight may not be a big deal for youngsters, in 1949 it was exciting for the boys to have a midnight ramble – with, of course, permission from their parents.

Ralph also arranged evenings at Detmold Road School to which a speaker would be invited and refreshments provided. Believing that such things should be done in style and that members should acquire the art of entertaining guests, these occasions were used as training in how to welcome visitors – as lessons in social skills. With members he arranged good food, good crockery – and good presentation. No mugs and biscuits here – it had to be china crockery (which Ralph would bring with him) and cakes.

Although there was a large membership by then, Ralph got to know the members individually and was always approachable and ready to give help and advice when needed. He did a great deal of work behind the scenes, helping members with their problems – often with their problems outside the club. He visited members' homes if required and gained the goodwill of many of their parents. He was close and supportive so that when two of the members were chosen to represent Great Britain in the Maccabiah Games in Israel, he went with them.

Part of Ralph's philosophy was that no member was bad – a view which was somewhat strained by one incident involving a small group of boys who were very troublesome, noisy, badly behaved and disruptive. Though the Club Committee wanted them banned, Ralph persisted. He said they needed to be encouraged, to be helped, that they were no different from any other members and must be allowed to stay. One evening the committee met with Ralph in the upstairs room. The meeting went on for some time and the committee was persuaded by Ralph to allow the boys to stay. When they came back into the club they discovered that the boys concerned had taken the piano to pieces!

Ralph was also fun. At fancy dress parties he would dress up, on one occasion – a Purim party – coming in a boy scout's uniform in very short shorts. (He was a tall man!)

After three years Ralph left to work for the Jewish Deaf Association. With his insight into the needs of the members and his innovations (particularly the move to Detmold Road School and the use of LCC instructors), he had made a great impact on the club's development. By setting the high standards which continued to be striven for throughout the club's life he contributed enormously to its success and progress.

Proof of the esteem in which Ralph was held and of his popularity was shown in 1993 when he returned to England from the United States where he had been living and working for many years. More than forty former members who had not seen him since he left the club in 1951 organised a special party for him so that they could meet him again.

Looking back, what I would have done different now is to get a further involvement of the community. We were getting by on a shoestring and people, the neighbourhood, could have afforded to support us better. Even the synagogue which gave us the premises really never quite accepted us. I didn't know how to sell us to the synagogue or to the neighbourhood (though) at least we were tolerated. Part of it was my fault. Somewhere or other I should have been at meetings of the boards of the synagogue and presented us as being part of and involved with them so that we would have had their blessing – and their cash. We did things without money.

From an interview with Ralph Goldstaub, club leader, 1948–51

Eva Levy (1951–54)

With a membership of 250, through the efforts mainly of the Parents' Association, the club was in a position in 1951 to employ another full-time worker and Ralph was joined by a girls' club leader, Eva Levy. She was a product of the Oxford and St George's Settlement and had been an experienced relief worker on the continent during the dreadful post-war years. While she and Ralph were very different personalities, they worked well together and the club continued to prosper. When Ralph left she worked equally well with his successors, David Davies and Lou Rose, concentrating on the needs of the girls.

> **Eva was a good leader. She wasn't married and her approach to the members – they were her children. She showed authority, taught us discipline and commonsense and decency. If she did not agree with what we wanted, she wouldn't allow us to do it and she stood her ground. She did gain our respect at the end of the day.**
> *Interview with male member/manager, 1949–57*

David Davies (1951–53)

David was a very orthodox young man who stayed two years and did much to maintain the orthodox and educational standards of the large membership. He arranged interesting programmes and demanded high standards of religious observance which were particularly enforced on club holidays. The members were not always happy with the number of services conducted on the holidays but they reluctantly took part out of respect for David's sincere observance.

Lou Rose (1953–60)

Henry Koor's comment to me on my son Alan's way of sharing me with 20 other children had made Lou and I take a good look at ourselves – at club or family and which should come first. We had been 'living club' for five years and were getting more and more involved in meetings and outside activities. In 1951, we therefore made the decision that family should come first and resigned from the club.

However, this turned out to be a short-lived decision. Very soon our two children became involved in the club themselves. Then Lou – who in 1946 had been the club's first voluntary leader – progressed from doing this full time to become full-time club leader. We were back to square one!

Lou continued in the job until 1960 and with Eva Levy was to take the club into the new premises. As it is obviously difficult for me to write about Lou, I have drawn on comments made at the time or on ones made on tape or in letters by former members and managers.

Lou, in the early days of the Clapton Club, gave up his time and patiently laid the foundation of what everyone must agree is an incredible record of sporting achievements! As a man he is quiet, unassuming and modest, and I hope I won't make him feel too old when I say, even fatherly to all the members. His few orations at the club were greeted with instant silence, which indicates undoubtedly the respect he commanded.
From a speech by a male club member (1946–52) at an event in 1952 to honour Lou Rose as a sportsman

Lou was always popular – he wanted always to do what we wanted him to do. He would very rarely say no to us, and we knew that. If (the girls club leader) did not think it was right, she didn't want to do it. But if Lou didn't think it was right and enough people wanted to do it, he'd give in. You know he was Mr Popularity itself – he really was a nice bloke. He understood and he certainly didn't seem 40 when we were involved with him – he seemed a lot younger because he had fantastic drive and energy, he really did. He would put his arm round you or clip you for your success, and it would be the same pat and arm round and clip for the unsuccessful. The well dones were just as strong for those who didn't make it as they were for the ones who did make it.
Interview with male member/manager, 1949–57

Lou not only guided the highly successful sporting activities, but by his calm steady presence gave every member a feeling of safety and security.
Letter from a male member, 1946–52

One learns from one's mentors, and undoubtedly a great deal of inspiration came from both of you during my formative years at the club. I have fond memories of those days, (and particularly of both of you)
Letter from a male member/manager, 1957–68

I remember being a little apprehensive at the club being orthodox. However my fears were quickly overcome mostly thanks to Lou's open-mindedness and willingness to try out some new and rather revolutionary ideas that I had brought forward.
Letter from Norman Spector, manager, 1956–63

Lou for me is the most unchanging person in that he is always there for you … He was no different on that first day from all the days ever onwards … Every time I was with Lou I felt I was with a father … he helped me so much … We were there in the club nearly every morning talking about everything that needed to be done for the evening, preparing. He was so diligent and he helped (me) to see … the way it should be done and the way I should be with the youngsters and in that sense I found it very easy because he was there constantly by my side but never intruding, never intrusive …

Interview with Jean Hersh, club leader 1956–59

Lou created a certain something which has persisted throughout the 23 years, and that is the friendly atmosphere for which the club is famous. Lou's effect and presence was so greatly felt that one former member recalls: 'If one saw Lou standing in the club smoking his pipe then everything was alright.'

Club magazine article written by two female club members, 1969

We had various club leaders come and go but they all pale into insignificance compared to Uncle Lou. I think a lot of things that we did or didn't do – to many of us it was important how he thought of us, and

• *'If one saw Lou … smoking his pipe then everything was alright.'*

many of the things we might have done I assume that we didn't do because we wouldn't have wanted him to be disappointed in us. He was very important.

Interview with female member, 1962–67

In 1960 Lou retired as full-time club leader but continued his active work in the club and then became activities officer at the AJY, still maintaining a close link with Clapton.

Jean (Hersh) Taylor (1956–59)

In 1956 the club took the decision to appoint its girls' club captain, Jean Hersh, as club leader. At that time Jean was only 18.

> **I don't think there was any real difficulty in becoming club leader ... There was no problem about Jean having been a club member (one day) and then being the club leader. That's how it all was at Clapton. I can't remember there being any hierarchical structure that said one day you are a club member, the next day you are not. It all went very smoothly. The transition wasn't difficult.**
> *Interview with Jean Hersh, club leader, 1956–59*

Having already been so much part of the club for some time, Lou and Jean turned out to be an effective team. They took the club through a time of great success, both internally and in all spheres of the club world beyond.

Jean, whose great interest was drama, encouraged a range of cultural activities – drama, art, public speaking – while Lou continued to draw on his enthusiasm for sport. Together they created a warm and friendly atmosphere and successfully coordinated all the work demanded by the varied aspects of club life.

After Jean left Clapton, she qualified as a drama teacher and now specialises in reminiscence therapy. She travels all over England and abroad, lecturing and tutoring on courses for workers in hospitals and residential homes for the elderly.

Joan and Leon Pratt (1961–64)

When Joan and Leon were appointed as part-time leaders for the junior club only, for the first time almost since it started the club was without full-time leadership. They were popular leaders who kept up a happy atmosphere in among the juniors, organising sporting activities and outings.

The rest of the club was run by a team of senior club members who had acquired know-how of the procedures and who carried out all the activities and administration. They were a splendid group of young people who worked very hard and cooperated well and happily together. They liaised with the Parents' Committee, the outside organisations and spent every evening at the club. However, the absence of a full-time leader was evident. Apart from the volume of work involved, a leader was needed to be there for members to turn to and to coordinate the work of managers and members.

Leon Rogers (1965–68)

An ex-member of the Brady Boys' Club, Leon was our first post-Albemarle leader following the publication of the report in 1960 which had such a radical effect on youth work and club leadership. He came to the club straight from the National College for the Training of Youth Leaders in Leicester which, on Albemarle's recommendation, had been set up in 1961 to train people as professional leaders. He was thus one of the first of a new generation of leaders who were changing the nature of leadership with their emphasis on groupwork and with participation as the 'in' word. We continued to help and worked well with Leon, though now without the joint responsibility we had shared with the former leaders.

Leon was a very good organiser who delegated well and created excellent members' committees. He recalls that the democracy created by the committees and the responsibilities they took on were so great that it allowed him to devote his time to groupwork and individual work with members. He also carried on the club's sporting tradition and encouraged many outside art and cultural activities, with members providing excellent entries into arts festivals and drama competitions.

However, the membership was changing and Leon, with his experience and training, was well aware of this. The age for the junior club was lowered from 10 to 8. He also encouraged members to go on training courses and was keen that the older ones take part in voluntary service – though he stressed that, to be effective, this had to be spontaneous and done on members' own initiative. Members helped at the Hackney Hospital on Christmas day and regularly visited elderly people.

Leon maintained very good personal relationships and was always ready to help members. He left in 1968 to become youth director of the Oxford and St George's Settlement.

Jack Langham (1968–72)

With membership now smaller, the club again reverted to part-time leadership. Jack had been for many years a LCC table tennis coach and so was well known to and popular with the members. He was efficient and enthusiastic as was evident from the fact that club week in 1970 raised the £375 needed to install central heating in the club.

Jack also appreciated that the nature of the membership was changing as were the needs of the young people using the club. Significantly, in 1971 Jesselo, Italy was the members' choice for a holiday – with hotel accommodation!

VOLUNTEERS

PARENTS AS VOLUNTEERS

In the old buildings, the managers – the people who, as volunteers, did most of the actual work with the members – were mainly parents. In the new building, they carried on loyally and enthusiastically (as did the LCC instructors). They came with a wide range of skills – and from a variety of backgrounds. Celia Levy, for example, sister of one of the members who ran a drama group, was a speech therapist who took choral speaking. Mr Sowter, a business man, took stamp collecting. With Mr Gnessen, a jeweller by trade, Mr Sowter also ran a handicraft group. Mrs Sowter, and Mrs Berliner (a parent) ran a needlework group for the girls, who would bring their own materials and make articles of clothing for themselves.

> **BEGINNERS BILLIARDS**
> **This group, under the instruction of Mr Herman, has really taught members to play and they have shown their worth in a number of inter-club tournaments, so if you still cannot play, here is your chance to learn.**
> *Club magazine, 1947*

Though without training in youth work, like Mr Herman (also a parent), they worked hard for the club, communicated well with members and endeared members to them. Many are still remembered with affection.

NEW RECRUITS

> **Clapton has not yet become the fashionable club towards which North West Londoners gravitate in a desire to become managers. Indeed, the centre has a minimum of adult help.**
> *From the AJY magazine,* Jewish Youth, *no 12, 1952*

Despite this rather gloomy view, as a result of the publicity it was getting and with its reputation growing, the club also began to attract younger people as managers. For example:

- Norma Yellin did not live in the district but had enquired about doing voluntary work and had been recommended to Clapton by Monty Richardson, a well-known Brady and AJY worker. She was a teaching graduate and took a drama group.
- Yogi Mayer, the leader of the Brady Club in the East End, asked Clapton to accept three young men for training as managers for his club – Cyril Kornfield, Bernie Schneider and Len Carton. They came for six months, stayed five years and proved to be excellent workers, particularly in sport.
- Pam and Norman Spector, who married after meeting at the club, also came through recommendations and were both managers for several years.

In 1956, when I was 24, I had the feeling that I wanted to do some voluntary club work and I offered my services to the AJY. I met with Mick Goldstein, the general secretary, and Sidney Drage, chairman of the Training Committee ... They suggested Clapton since it wasn't too far to travel and was well established with a good leader (our dear Lou), and Doris Benson, a girls' club leader ... remember being a little apprehensive at the club being on the premises of an orthodox synagogue, (and I can hardly describe myself as being orthodox!). However, my fears were quickly overcome ...

We had a marvellous group of seniors, 16+ at the time – very bright kids who had a far greater potential than just doing sports and jiving. Slowly, slowly, we started bringing interesting and provocative speakers to the club. We had a Reform Rabbi who was thrown out of South Africa for denouncing apartheid from his pulpit. We also had political speakers from the main parties. We had musicians playing chamber music and all sorts of things. Personally, I got great satisfaction to see the room full of lovely bright teenagers firing questions at the speakers which were sometimes hard for them to answer. Claire Rayner, a friend of my sister, was at the club at this time: she was a nurse and writing newspaper articles, but we were certainly her first speaking platform ...

I think that on some occasions I spent more time at the club than at home. This younger group of managers became a social group and whilst enjoying the work at the club, enjoyed the friendships, many of which have lasted a lifetime.
Letter from Norman Spector, manager, 1956–63

After partaking in an AJY course, I was sent to Clapton from the Willesden Synagogue Club. I took the girls for deportment, talks about growing up, clothes, make up, attitudes, etc. I also remember playing rounders in the playing fields next to the club, it was great fun. I travelled from South East London twice a week to Clapton, and very much enjoyed working at the club.

After about a year at the club, I decided I would like to qualify as a club leader, and went to Israel on the 'Machon' course – a year's youth leadership training. When I came back, I went to see May Mundy (Training and Development Officer at the time) at the AJY as she had encouraged me through the training courses. I was very surprised to find that ... my year in Israel did not count in professional qualifications. So I went back to the secretarial work (and) was accepted as a voluntary leader at Clapton and worked with Norman. We ... stayed until we emigrated to Israel in 1963.

Letter from Pam Spector, manager, 1957–63

Although not all of them had had previous experience in youth work, they too brought a range of skills and enthusiasm.

FROM MEMBER TO MANAGER

The club maintained a hold on me, and I came back to help ... I don't seem to recall much of this. The probability is that I did it so as not to lose the magic of those years, but, of course, things are never the same.

Letter from male club member, 1951–57

The founder members' experience on club and AJY committees and of carrying responsibility meant that many of them stayed on as managers at Clapton and at other clubs. They too brought a great breadth of experience and skill to the club and made a valuable contribution. Several of them took AJY and club training courses (see pages 63–66) and in due course used their various skills as managers. Their potential showed at an early age. One member who always excelled in public speaking and essay competitions demonstrated this at the age of 15, even before he had been involved in any training.

DEBATING GROUP

Martin Compton wants to start a debating society for the boys, to be held fortnightly, where every member can 'air' his views on any subject he may wish to choose. If you are interested, give him your name and the subject you wish to be debated, so that he may start organising it as soon as possible.
Club magazine, 1948

Martin, now a solicitor, stayed at the club until he was married. As well as helping with activities and conducting the youth service, at a later date he became chairman of the club.

We were also lucky to find some volunteers who worked in the arts and drama, and the AJY and national associations offered competition. We were able to reach a completely new standard in our participation in dramatic events, in essay writing, in all sorts of intellectual activities, enabling the club to achieve very many successes,
From an interview with Ralph Goldstaub, club leader,1948–51

EXTERNAL TRAINING

Courses

The main source of training for volunteers through the '50s and '60s were the courses provided by the AJY Clubs' Advisory and Training and Development Committees. The leading people on these committees at that time were Sidney Drage, Monty Richardson and Charles Spencer, all key workers at the Brady Club. Dr Wendy Greengross, a practising GP and a specialist in counselling, also worked closely with the committees. These were serviced from the AJY by May Mundy and Sidney Bunt, training and development officers who both took an active part in the programmes.

Training courses for club workers and senior members were run as residential events over full weekends (Friday evening to Sunday afternoon). They were held at Skeet, the Brady Club's country house at Swanley in Kent, and at the Sir Max Bonn Centre at Bracklesham Bay near Chichester in Sussex. Day courses were also organised at the larger clubs in London.

An important part of these experiences for the younger people was getting to know the tutors, meeting and socialising with members from other clubs, making friends and exchanging views. However, Sidney Drage, a most imaginative trainer, made the courses themselves exciting, meaningful and fun (it was he who introduced role play into the training).

So too did Wendy Greengross whose training approach emphasised personal relationships. She encouraged those taking part to talk freely about themselves, their motives in the work they were doing in their clubs, their feelings, doubts and worries, and their attitudes. Though all this was sometimes quite painful and could only have been dealt with by such an experienced counsellor, groups learnt a great deal from each other.

Henry Shaw was AJY's religious director working with another of its committees, the Religious Advisory Committee. He was a good friend and advisor to Clapton, visited the club often, gave talks and took part in discussions. He also organised the oratory and essay competitions in which Clapton took a very active part.

With his wife, Sybil, he took a girls' group to Bracklesham Bay in 1951 where, as part of an enjoyable holiday, they learnt songs and were instructed on the lighter side of Jewish education.

• *AJY oratory competition 1951, pictured left to right: Barbara Nathan, Harold Margolis and Martin Compton.*

From the early years, the importance of helping others and taking responsibility was stressed in the club. With the help of the courses run by AJY, many Clapton members developed into excellent managers, not only at Clapton itself but at other clubs. For example, one 16-year-old member who had learnt Israeli dancing taught a group in the junior club at Clapton and in 1953 went to Hackney Club to teach a similar group there. In 1955 two Clapton members aged 17 and 18 became managers at a newly-formed club for 10 to 14-year-olds in the nearby Boundary Road Synagogue where they took a drama group. Indeed, after they married, several former Clapton members became managers in clubs in the areas to which they had moved.

AJY MEMBERS' COUNCIL

The AJY sponsored a Members' Council for 16 to 18-year-olds. Two members of each club were elected with more being able to attend without having a vote. Training weekends were organised for council members as well as social activities and an annual conference. The council was represented on the AJY's Executive Committee which had overall responsibility for the Association's policy, finance and administration and on its three divisional committees for under 13s, under 16s and under 19s. (In 1960 the Members' Council was renamed Members' Parliament.)

Clapton always had members on the council who enjoyed their programmes enormously. It also gave them good experience in taking responsibilities and produced many helpers/managers for the club.

AJY ANNUAL CONFERENCE

Each year, at one of the larger East London Clubs, a dinner was held on Saturday evening with a keynote speaker. It was an important social event – one of the highlights of the club year also attended by leaders, managers, other voluntary workers and chairmen. The conference then took place all day on the Sunday – with the same people attending. There were workshops which sometimes followed up the speaker's theme from the previous evening and plenary sessions. The format varied – in some years a panel ended the day to answer questions. This gave members, leaders and voluntary workers an opportunity to mix and learn from each other.

LONDON UNION OF YOUTH CLUBS

In 1969, the London Union of Youth Clubs introduced a scheme to encourage drama in clubs. They offered seats for the shows to members who were involved in drama groups at affordable prices. These, normally costing 32s 6d, were available for 5s. Through this scheme members saw Laurence Olivier in *Othello* and *Dance of Death*, both at the National Theatre; *Belchers Luck* at the Aldwich; *Loot* at the Criterion and many plays at the Old Vic.

IN-SERVICE TRAINING

From the club's early years senior members went to smaller clubs to help run activities such as Israeli dancing and junior activities as well as to larger clubs to get a wider experience. In addition, during the time he was club leader, Ralph Goldstaub arranged weekend training courses just for Clapton managers and senior members. These were held at Leigh House, Bracklesham Bay and, as well as allowing internal matters to be discussed, provided wider training on such things as personal relationships, attitudes and social skills.

Clapton training courses were also run over a period of several weeks in 1972 by Sheila Dainow, a Stamford Hill worker who specialised in counselling and training. These were well attended sessions which resulted in some senior members offering help to small clubs which were short of helpers. Some of those taking part also went to larger clubs to get further training under the supervision of full-time professional leaders.

A further important aspect of the training offered within the club to managers and senior members was the example set by the leaders and other managers – how well they cooperated, their understanding of the work and of members, their ability to give members space and encouragement to develop their own talents and potential leadership.

'MOULDING TRUE AND CONSCIENTIOUS JEWS AND JEWESSES'

Today we can be proud that (we) not only have a club that gives its members group activities and outdoor sports ... but also a Jewish Club where we feel we are being moulded into true and conscientious Jews and Jewesses.

Editorial, club magazine, April 1947

We are Jewish boys and girls, and by practising the fundamentals of Judaism, which are tolerance, humility and mercy, we will not only have gained, but we will have earned the praise and respect of the nation. And I do feel that Clubs should train members in Judaism, for in this country where it is predominantly Christian, we are apt to err, and there arises the serious question of inter-marriage which is a difficult problem which has to be faced.

Female club member, 1946–54: first prize, AJY under 19s Oratory Competition, 1949

Before I became a Clapton member, I thought club life consisted of table-tennis, draughts and things like that. I have since learnt not only how to hold a table-tennis bat, and what the next move in draughts is, but to love and respect my religion.

Female club member, 1949–55: first prize, AJY under 16s Oratory Competition, 1949

More than anything else in this thrilling short story of Clapton's growth has been the philosophy of its development. Too many clubs growing in the new Jewish areas away from the East End had no particular views on their spiritual function. In Clapton there was to be a new approach – to use the best East End club techniques and also to state proudly and unequivocally that every aspect of the club would be devoted to the furtherance and fostering of traditional Judaism – not merely paying lip service to these ideals.

From the AJY magazine, Jewish Youth, *no 12, 1952*

> **For me it was my Jewish contact, after all at school as I said I didn't have any Jewish contact and it also helped me work out in a sense my Jewishness because the Jewish identity at the club was one that was defined.**
>
> *Interview with male club member, 1950–58*

THE CLUB, THE SYNAGOGUE AND THE AJY

The generally harmonious relationship which the club had with the Clapton Synagogue throughout its existence was best demonstrated by its free use of synagogue premises. Synagogue members were proud of the club's success and of its status in the community. However, though the synagogue was represented on the Club Council and its officers attended all the club functions, they rarely visited the club while it was in session. They were content to allow it to function without any interference on their part – one reason, no doubt, for the survival of the good relationship.

> **The fact that you are holding your activities in our premises does not only show that you are our good neighbours and friends, but we see in the close ties that have developed between the two of us a much greater thing ...**
>
> **We want to provide your club with a real home, as only parents can do for a child. That does not mean that we want to boss you in any way; you know you are independent and your own free agents in every aspect of club life ...**
>
> **We need you as much as you need us. Let us stick together. We all have one aim: to be good Jews, and true and useful citizens of the country.**
>
> *Rabbi Dr D. Lewin, club magazine, April 1947*

In the late '40s the AJY set up a group to study the best ways of introducing Jewish culture into the clubs. As a result a Religious Advisory Committee was formed with representatives from all the synagogue bodies. They all gave financial support to a scheme for appointing club ministerial officers to clubs, though the main financial contributor was the United Synagogue through its Welfare Committee. They also organised training weekends.

The title ministerial officer was derived from a pre-war scheme for students in their last year at Jews College who were living in the Buxton

Street Welfare Centre in East London. They had been attached to AJY clubs so that they could gain wider experience before they qualified.

Over the years Clapton, where a traditional Jewish atmosphere was always the focal part of the work, recruited three of these officers from within the club. The first was Maurice Berenblutt whose work is described below; the second Martin Compton (already mentioned as an active committee member who, in 1965, became chairman of the club) and the third Jeffrey Leifer, a member and then a manager who devoted an enormous amount of time and energy to the club throughout most its life.

The religious director of the AJY, Henry Shaw, who once described his job as 'selling religion' which is most difficult, was another person who contributed a great deal to Clapton's religious life as a club in the period 1949 to 1955. He was a regular visitor and a good and popular friend who was also responsible for arranging the AJY oratory and essay competitions in which Clapton always took part.

RELIGIOUS SERVICES

I tried orthodox (Judaism) when I was about 17, but it didn't last for more than about three weeks because I found it clashed with Spurs playing on a Saturday ...
Interview with male club member/manager, 1946–52

Services for children

In May 1948 a children's Sabbath morning service was started in the old club building, led by two 14-year-old club members Martin Compton and Cyril Brill.

These services ... are attended by over 70 boys and girls every Sabbath. We are pleased to note that more and more of the service is being taken over by the boys and girls themselves. They are conducted both in Hebrew and English and are very easy to follow and understand.
Club magazine, April 1948

It outgrew these premises very quickly and in 1949 moved to the local Millfields Road School. Here, under the auspices of the United Synagogue, an officiant was appointed, Arnold Cohen. With Arnold closing his eyes to the fact that a big attraction was the game of football which took place in the school grounds before the service started, 200 children were soon attending, their ages (including their younger sisters and brothers) ranging between 3 and 14. Another attraction was the orange squash and cake, served after the service!

As these services were considered educational, it had been decided in 1948 that they should be linked more closely to the club. As a result, attendance at the Sabbath morning service became a condition of becoming a junior (that is, under 13) club member, and remained so for many years. Though they were shorter than the synagogue service, the children's service gave the officiant a chance to explain to the younger members the meaning of the service and to teach them how to take part. They did not object – and their parents were delighted.

These Sabbath morning services carried on until 1960 when, as the numbers began to drop, they moved back to the club. Michael Levy, then aged 16, became the officiant for some seven years. He also formed a choir which took part in the AJY music festivals. With other club members taking over, the services for children carried on until the club closed.

The High Holy Days children's services (the Jewish New Year and the Day of Atonement), which often fell on weekdays, were taken by

• *Alan Gilby at a youth service, 1952.*   • *Ralph Goldstaub, club leader, officiating at a religious service.*

Arnold Cohen and were held in St James Hall, a local church hall. With attendances frequently reaching nearly three hundred, Frances Bookatz, a 15-year-old club member, separated off the under 8s for a service on their own. These services carried on until the early '60s.

Youth services

In 1951 a full Sabbath service for the over 13s was started at the club by Cyril Brill and Martin Compton, now aged 17, with members taking part. They also conducted a service for the High Holy Days – something which was said at the time by the AJY religious director to be unique to Clapton. Martin and Cyril continued to take the services until they married (in 1960 and 1961) and moved out of the district. The services continued to be carried on by two other members, Martin Whitefield and Michael Levy.

During this period, when the old house was being pulled down in 1953, the Sabbath morning Youth Service moved to the B'nei Akivah Bayit (House) in Cazenove Road and was taken by Frances Bookatz. She continued to officiate when the new building was established in 1954 for about two years, but the synagogue then decided there was an objection to a female and a decision was taken that a male should officiate.

> **You had to go to services in order to become a club member – that strikes me as outrageous now but those were things that I guess I didn't understand very well at the time or at least I wasn't in a position to question.**
> *Interview with male club member, 1950–58*

> **I had, of course, been to Shul before, but quite frankly the services had been a little meaningless. At the club I was introduced to a regular weekly youth service which I found I could understand.**
> *'What my club meant to me', club magazine, 1957, by male club member, 1946–55*

Special Services

In March 1956, its 10th anniversary, the club held a service taken by the members. Members, parents and a large congregation of distinguished visitors filled the synagogue.

CELEBRATING THE JEWISH FESTIVALS

The Clapton club always celebrated the Jewish festivals in grand style. The object was to present traditional religion in a new light and make it meaningful, exciting and at the same time educational. The religious observances were carried out actually within the club and large parties organised by the Parents' Association. Representatives of the synagogue would attend and also VIPs from organisations connected with the club.

On the Festival of Succoth, for example (the Harvest Festival), the canteen would be turned into a Succah (a tent-like structure). Although this was supposed to have an open roof and be covered in boughs, members found it fun to decorate and created the atmosphere of the festival. The Festival of Chanukah (the Festival of Lights), which is celebrated over eight days, was another highlight in the club year. Members made their own Menorot (candelabrum) by reconstructing the original oil lamp and, with the help of the art teacher, designed a collage symbolising the Battle of the Macabees.

CHANUKAH PARTY
The Chanukah party ... was a huge success. Almost our entire membership of 100 arrived in good time ... After tea we had dancing and games. Their worships the Mayor and Mayoress joined in all the fun ... The parents then began to arrive and were served refreshments ... The second part of the evening opened with Stanley Appel and Bernard Rochlin kindling the Chanukah lights. We were then entertained by a delightful concert party ... For the last part of the evening ... Rev Rashbass spoke to us with complete understanding of youth, explaining the significance of the Chanukah festival ...
Club magazine, April 1947

FANCY DRESS AND ANNIVERSARY PARTY
If you happened to walk into the club a few weeks before Purim you would have been sure to hear someone say 'What are you going to wear?' or 'You want to see my costume?' and if you stayed a little longer you would have gathered that everyone was preparing for our Purim and First Anniversary Party. Well, they arrived, and it seemed as if nearly all our members had either changed their nationality, their sex, or their professions ...
Club magazine, April 1947

RELIGIOUS EDUCATION WITHIN THE CLUB

Religious education featured in the club programme from the beginning. After the club moved to its new premises, religious education was encouraged by one of the managers, Morrie Berunblut. Using the canteen which was open all evening, he would just 'be there' before and after activities when members congregated for refreshments and to socialise. A very sincere orthodox young man with a sympathetic understanding of young people, he would sit and chat with members, listen to their views and encourage them to talk freely without judging them or trying to impose his own views. This was true even if they told him that they were apathetic to religion or did not believe. Some of the members came from unobservant homes so that, with the club's emphasis on religion, they needed to be able to voice their feelings and, sometimes, their frustrations and uncertainties. Because Morrie was well-liked and respected, members have said that he helped them and had an influence on them.

Morrie also introduced the Oneg Shabbat to the club – the Sabbath afternoon gathering – when a group would meet at a member's house for songs and discussion and to review the Sidra (the week's reading at the synagogue service). The meetings were followed by tea and attracted the more serious-minded members. Though usually held in the vicinity of the club, one Saturday the meeting was at our own house involving a three-mile walk. They arrived so exhausted we thought they had walked a marathon!

> **ONEG SHABBAT**
> **Atmosphere friendly and informal, the procedure being controlled entirely by club members. We hope to widen the field and ask for suitable suggestions for future meetings. There is no formal committee as each member is asked to play their part in the organisation and running of what we feel is an essential club activity. Attendance has been very good; however, the bulk are members who visited Israel this year and we feel it is important that the remainder of the club should develop an interest in this matter.**
> *Club magazine, 1958*

THE HOLOCAUST

In the period immediately after the war the horrors of the Holocaust were emerging. In recent years a great deal has been written and educational programmes have been devised for young people to make sure they understand what happened in Europe and that the subject is introduced into the schools curriculum.

However, though no doubt there were Clapton members whose parents had lost relatives and friends in Europe, we did not seem to be aware of this in the club. Even though it was so close to the Jews at that time, no efforts were made to educate the members about the events leading up to the war and the catastrophe which followed for both the Jews and many non-Jews, nor about the importance and effects of the Holocaust for them as Jews. In retrospect, it is very painful that during all the years the club was running so little apparently was done to make members aware of the impact of this devastating part of Jewish history.

ZIONISM

On the other hand, in line with how most Jews felt after the war and indeed over the life of the club, and like most AJY-affiliated clubs, support for Israel was very much taken for granted at Clapton. Passing comments, for example in club magazines and members' speeches in oratory competitions, sometimes made this very clear.

> **We are standing on the eve of a very great epoch in the history of our people with the realisation of our dream in having a state of our own. We, the Jewish youth in this country, must try and find the best way in helping towards this tremendous task and at the same time help to strengthen the Jewish community in England.**
> *By Henry Koor, club leader, 1947–49, in the club magazine, 1948*

> **The last catastrophic war divided children from their parents ... These conditions left a gap in their young lives which was the most impressionable years for a youth. The Jewish club has set itself the colossal task of filling the gap in young Israel ...**
> *First prize speech in AJY under 16s Oratory Competition, 1948, by female member, 1947–55*

> **... we the Jewish people, we who have suffered, we who have only just found our home after two thousand years, we know the need for tolerance.**
> *First prize speech in under 19s AJY Oratory Competition, 1948, by female member, 1946–52*

The belief in Zionism also came through in club events and activities. For example, during the 1947–48 period, Shoshana and Moishe Portnoi – a young couple affectionately known as Shosh and Mosh who were leaders with the Bnei Akivah (an orthodox Zionist movement) – took a group of juniors for Hebrew singing and dancing on Saturday afternoons. And other more direct contacts were made with Zionist youth groups.

> **On Sunday June 8th a coach party of twenty-five members and six managers visited Bachad Farm at Thaxted. The farm ... is completely run and cultivated by the young men and young women who are training there in preparation for their emigration to Palestine. The farm is run on the lines of the Kibbutzim in Palestine ... All money is pooled and money needed for clothes and amusements are taken from the pool ... We finished the day watching the young folk enjoying their well earned leisure time by having a game of football ...**
> *Club magazine, April 1948*

Most significant perhaps was the club's visit to Israel in 1958 (see The club away from home, pages 115–117). This was prompted by the success of a visit in 1957 by an AJY party of club workers which included the Clapton leader Jean Hersh, a former leader Eva Levy and a Clapton manager Norman Spector as well as many leading personalities in Jewish youth work. They came back so impressed with everything they had seen and experienced that Clapton immediately started to plan a club visit. With Stamford Hill, Clapton thus became the first youth group not attached to a Zionist movement to go to Israel under the sponsorship of the Jewish Agency which, among other responsibilities, encouraged such contacts. The visit did a great deal to promote interest in Israel among club members, to such an extent that many of them returned for holidays and some returned to settle.

Some leaders did not support Zionism and even gave the impression of being anti-Zionist. In 1948, the year the State of Israel was declared, a motion was proposed at an AJY Annual General Meeting of about two hundred people that it should be sent a message of greetings. An amendment was proposed by three leading figures in youth work nationally who ran large Jewish youth centres that greetings be sent to Jews in other countries. The redoubtable Miriam Moses poured scorn on their efforts to belittle the welcome to the new State and the amendment was overwhelmingly defeated, thereby confirming what we had known already: that, though the AJY may not have been a Zionist movement, we were certainly not anti-Zionist.

CLAPTON'S JEWISH ETHOS

Looking back some former members indicated some mixed feelings about the club's strong Jewish ethos.

> **Perhaps the idea of being so closely Jewish doesn't fit you for accepting the multi-cultural atmosphere that we have today ... It didn't give us a problem (then) ... it was right at the time so soon after the war. But I would like to see a club (now) not exclusively Jewish but more ... all embracing. There are things to be said for both ways. It helps the local community to develop if there is that closeness ... (But) I would always like to feel that people from different cultural backgrounds can mix well ... I think people perhaps have to develop within their own culture first and then branch out to be confident. You develop a confidence because you have been accepted amongst equals.**
> *Interview with male and female club members, 1946–52*

> **The philosophy of the club ... probably fitted in with the Jewish social interests of the time which was very separatist. It didn't encourage people to mix with non-Jews at all – in fact it positively discouraged members to be affable to non-Jewish girls in the club.**
> *Interview with male club member/manager, 1946–52*

> **... as I look back I think it was very narrow for example ... (the) mixture of religion and social events was very heavily weighted in favour of religion ... Even if people didn't keep the laws they wouldn't have questioned the idea of believing in God. You would never have described anyone in the club as a Jewish atheist ...**

> **It becomes very delicate and difficult to discuss the boundaries of being Jewish ... to encourage Jewish identity while at the same time opening up different ideas of what a Jew is.**
> *Interview with male club member, 1950–58*

However, the members who made these comments were expressing as they feel today. At the time they were actually in the club they were happy to accept it as an all-Jewish club while their parents were certainly pleased that their children's leisure time was being spent in an all-Jewish environment.

Indeed, for many members their club experience was a way for them to work out their identification in regard to their being Jewish.

DEVELOPING THE PROGRAMME – BECOMING A MIXED CLUB

People joined in everything ... everybody was doing something. You didn't see people standing around, just playing around – they were doing an activity.

Interview with Norma Yellin, drama instructor, 1955–57

THE CLUB AND THE AJY

While the internal groups and classes described earlier continued, many of the activities developed by the club were based around the Jewish festivals and on external competitions. Here, the London Union of Youth Clubs, the London Federation of Boys' Clubs and the Association for Jewish Youth (AJY) were essential sources of help, especially in the early years. The staff of the AJY particularly supported and encouraged the club throughout its history with the Association's programmes for all age groups enabling it to grow and develop.

The AJY developed out of the Jewish Athletic Association, formed in 1899 by a handful of pioneers who, as managers of clubs and officers of the Jewish Lads' Brigade, were dedicated to the service of youth. These idealists, mainly sons and daughters of some of Anglo-Jewry's leading families, believed that the future of the Jewish community in England was closely bound up with training its young people. Coming as they did from more privileged homes at a time when clubs were run by voluntary managers, they went into the East End imbued with the desire to pass on some of their own training to young Jews – girls as well as boys – who were less fortunately placed than themselves. In 1924 a Central Council of Jewish Boys' and Young Men's Institutes was also established which in due course merged with the Jewish Athletic Association in 1927 to form the AJY.

When the club affiliated to AJY in 1946, David Mellows was its general secretary. He was joined in 1949 by Mick Goldstein who succeeded him in l952 and remained with the Association for 32 years. (In 1967 Mick was awarded the MBE for his outstanding work for the youth service.)

> **I think Clapton was right for its time. It was sponsored by the synagogue and one would expect it to follow their requirements. Clapton was one of the last newly formed Jewish clubs, and there were a number in the post-war years, to affiliate to the London Union of Girls' Clubs and the London Federation of Boys' Clubs. They really availed themselves of the services of these organisations and the AJY in terms of training and in terms of the programming in the broadest level. This was good for the club and of course good for the parent organisations.**
>
> *Mick Goldstein, General Secretary, AJY, 1949–81*

CLUB AGE GROUPS AND PROGRAMME

Though at the club's peak the largest age group was probably the intermediates (the 13 to 16-year-olds), the club's membership was fairly evenly distributed between it and the other two sections – the juniors (10 to 13s), and the seniors (over 16s).

Opposite is a typical programme for the period – in this case 1951 – when, it needs to be remembered, a senior club was only just developing as the original members reached 16+.

SINGLE SEXED OR MIXED?

> **I came as a boys' club leader and I don't quite know where but we very much became a mixed club. I think the important thing the club did was teach boys and girls an appropriate way to relate to each other and the fact that so many of them married each other I think is proof that we did very well in teaching socialisation between the sexes.**
>
> *Interview with Ralph Goldstaub, club leader, 1948–51*

From the early days of Jewish youth work, girls and boys were kept separate – indeed, some of the clubs had separate buildings. This meant

MONDAY			
5 – 6	Hackney Baths	Juniors	Swimming, games
5 – 6	Club	Juniors	Games
6 – 7	Club	Juniors	Needlework, fretwork, dramatics, art
7 – 8	Club	Intermediates	Games
7.30 – 9.30	Detmold Road	Intermediates	Ballroom dancing class
8 – 9.30	Club	Intermediates	Group activities
9.30 – 10.30	Club	Intermediates	Social and canteen
TUESDAY			
7.30 – 9.30	Club	Intermediates	Discussion/study groups, stamp collecting
7.30 – 9.30	Detmold Road	Intermediates	Table tennis tournaments
9.30 – 10.30	Club	Intermediates	Social and canteen
WEDNESDAY			
7 – 8	Club	Intermediates	Discussion/study groups
7.30 – 9.30	Club	Intermediates	Music appreciation, photography
7.30 – 9.30	Detmold Road	Intermediates	Dramatics, art, handicraft (ceramics, modelling, fretwork)
9.30 – 10.30	Club	Intermediates	Social and canteen
THURSDAY			
8 – 9	Hackney Baths	Intermediates/Seniors	Swimming
7.30 – 9.30	Club	Seniors	Drama, discussion groups
7.30 – 9.30	Detmold Road	Intermediates	PT classes
9.30 – 10.30	Club	Intermediates/Seniors	Social and canteen
SUNDAY			
2.30 – 5.00	Club	Juniors	Hebrew dancing and singing
7 – 10.30	Club	Intermediates/Seniors	Social

Full programme of sport for all age groups
Monthly dance at Detmold Road during winter months

In addition to these programmed activities, games would also be available including chess and draughts and billiards.

• *Single sexed or mixed club?*

that a strong tradition of separate girls' activities existed from the start – for example, the first Jewish girls' club on Butler's Street, was founded in 1903 and remained an all-girls club until it closed in 1939. Brady Girls' Club, founded in 1925 in its own building, moved into the boys' club premises at Durward Street in 1928 and, despite some attempts at mixing, stayed separate. Indeed it moved into its own new building in 1935 and was only integrated with the boys' club, though still with some separate activities, in 1950.

Although some held out, older clubs too were becoming mixed – the Stepney Lads' Club merged with the Cambridge and Hackney Club in 1960. From the '50s and '60s, too, the smaller Jewish clubs which opened were mixed, leading to a general impression that the boys were getting a better deal, mainly because of the accent on sport.

> **To the question 'Is it a good thing that the Girls' Club has now given way to the Mixed Club?', Miss Moses (founder of Brady Girls' Club) said there is definitely something lost. Boys, being more club conscious, tend to over-rule the girls ... Mixed clubs will be predominant, but girls, take this advice from Miss Moses, stand up for yourselves – make sure that we women have our say, and that our views are respected.**
> *'All about Eve' by a female Clapton member, from the AJY magazine,* Jewish Youth, *1959*

> **Miss Gerson (Warden of Stepney Jewish Girls' Club) thinks it is only right that Mixed Clubs should take the place of Girls'**

Clubs, assuming that there is some provision for separate activities.

'All about Eve' by a female Clapton member, from the AJY magazine, Jewish Youth, *1959*

When Clapton started, it was part of the older tradition of separate provision. It had separate evenings for boys and girls with one mixed evening when socials were held. However, after about two years the boys were coming into the girls' evenings and vice versa. By popular demand from the members and by general agreement of the council, club committee and managers, the decision was taken by the Club Council that Clapton would become a mixed club.

However, at Clapton, as the girls on the Club Committee took equal responsibility, it was never male dominated. Also, single-sex activities continued – for example, the cookery and the sports teams, in particular netball, rounders, table tennis and swimming – and talks and

• *Girls' netball team, 1948.*

discussions were arranged on women's affairs, including the sessions on sex described in Cultural Activities and the Wider World, pages 91–98.

There were also girls-only competitions while the fashion shows, though mixed, involved mainly girls. Some of the club holidays, like the ones at Bracklesham Bay in the club's first three years, were just for girls – in 1951 Henry and Sibyl Shaw took a girls' group there, combining an educational programme with lots of fun.

I don't remember in all my years at the club feeling that the boys had a better deal than we had.

Interview with female club member, 1951–58

Nor was it just a matter of the girls taking part in the actual activities and events. They also enjoyed the social contact of being together. One

• Some of the holidays were just for girls, like the ones to Bracklesham Bay.

former female member recalls, for example, that travelling to matches was all part of the experience and that after playing netball in Bethnal Green on a Sunday, the team and supporters would go off together to Johnny Isaacs's in Whitechapel for chips.

Often just playing netball with the girls on a Sunday – we used to go together – those things I look back on as tremendously joyful times. We had such fun together and just being with those girls was also very very special for me. I think that taught me a great deal about being with women. I now love being with women ... I think I began to learn that there on the netball field on a Sunday afternoon ...
Interview with female member, 1950–55

GIRLS' HOLIDAY AT LEIGH HOUSE, BRACKLESHAM BAY
August 1947

On August 18th, eighteen excited girls with the Rose family boarded the coach that was about to take them to Bracklesham Bay for the summer holidays. Anxious parents stood by the coach giving their daughters last minute advice ... After sorting ourselves out into rooms of twos and fours, and unpacking, we ran across the garden to have our first real look at the sea. Then we had tea and soon afterwards most of us had our first glorious dip.

... As we had had a long and exciting day, we were expected to turn in early – well, we did go to bed fairly early, but after all, we had never slept four in a room before and had never been away without our parents, so it was too much to expect us to go to sleep. Mr and Mrs Rose were patrolling until late in the night trying to suppress excited giggling girls ...

• 'Our first glorious dip!'

The usual programme was, during the day, swimming and lazing on the beach. ... In between ... we had some very good games of cricket, rounders and physical jerks led by Mr Rose ... Some evenings we had sing-songs in the lounge overlooking the brightly moon-lit sea. I think we will always remember those lovely evenings and the spontaneous way all the girls – even the one-time shy ones – joined in and even sang solo.

Female member's report, club magazine, April 1948

The AJY also arranged non-sporting events for girls in which Clapton members took part. These included an early series of discussion groups for girls' representatives from clubs, sometimes with a guest speaker on matters relating to club problems and sometimes on more general subjects.

• Girls' holiday to Bracklesham Bay.

AJY GIRL MEMBERS' GATHERINGS

Each month the AJY arranges gatherings where a few members from each club come together and enjoy a discussion group ...The last one was held at our Club and the subject was 'The place of the Club in the Jewish community'. The gist of the discussion was that the Club's place was one of the training grounds where girls are trained to take their places in the future as good Jewish citizens and mothers.

Club magazine, April 1948

Again in the '50s and '60s the AJY ran girls' training weekends at Skeet Hill, the Brady Club holiday house. It also recognised the work of the girls by making an annual Rebecca Harris award. Rebecca Harris founded and devoted her life to the Lemon Street East London Girls' Club. As a tribute to her work, the AJY introduced this award in 1955, for a girl who had been a regular club attender and made the greatest contribution to her club. In 1956 it was won by Clapton member Elaine Waxman and in 1957 by Sally Rose.

SPORT AND SPORTSMANSHIP

'WIN OR LOSE – IT'S THE GAME THAT COUNTS'

I seem to recall being forced to move off the table tennis to join in discussion meetings in classrooms. Thereafter it was football, football and football. The Elms and Hackney Marshes: washing in cold water, travelling by bus and train, meeting up with team mates before we left for matches, and spending Sunday evenings at club dances ... talking about football because I was too shy to ask girls to dance.
Letter from male club member, 1951–57

I was mad on table-tennis and so was (my friend) ... Every Thursday night about 5 minutes before closing time (we) would call out 'Goodnight', slam the door closed and hush hush run downstairs to the cellar ... We would listen till Ralph went, wait a few minutes, come out of the basement, go upstairs, close all the shutters on the front. We would get the table-tennis table out and play till I or 2 o'clock in the morning. We did it every Thursday.
Interview with male club member, 1946–55

I went in for athletics but I wasn't especially good at it. But I did go in for it. I went in for everything sporting.
Interview with female club member, 1949–55

The AJY's sporting competitions were particularly (though, as we shall see, not only) important to the growth of the club programme. On an average Sunday a thousand members took part in AJY football leagues. Its annual swimming galas, over two very full afternoons, were equally well attended. In 1949 the annual AJY athletics meeting was held in three sessions, for under 14s, under 16s and under 19s as well as men and women. That year it attracted 840 competitors, rising during the decade from 1955 to 1965 to 1,000 (drawn from 1,200 to 1,600 entries).

• Football,
football,
football …!

Because of the great interest and enthusiasm which Lou had helped to create, sport continued to play a major part in club life at Clapton. A very full programme was offered which included football, cricket, tennis, netball, athletics, swimming, boxing and PT as well as indoor games such as table tennis and chess.

Some members and managers were always out to win at all costs. However, Lou's example helped to build a spirit of sportsmanship which emphasised that what was most important was taking part and the enjoyment this gave. In his instinctive way, he seemed to follow the philosophy of the late Ernest Halsted and Ernest Joseph, dedicated youth workers of the '50s. As set out in Charles L. Magnus's book *E.M. Joseph:*

• Cricketers and footballers, 1948.

The Man and His Work published in 1962, they 'shared the conviction that the sports field is an invaluable – indeed an essential – medium for training boys' characters.'

You have the makings of a fine team lads, stick to it but remember above all, win or lose, it's the game that counts. Just one word of advice – please try and make a little less noise on the field. Best of luck for next season.

Mr L. Rose, club magazine, April 1947

This spirit was particularly in evidence at AJY annual sports days held at the different athletics tracks – Victoria Park in Hackney, Parliament Hill Fields in north west London or in Wimbledon. A whole bank of Clapton supporters would turn up, with banners, to cheer on the teams and have a good time. In the process, members, parents and managers from different clubs got to know each other, creating a friendship among them. Even in bad weather, the same crowds would be there, huddled under umbrellas, showing their loyalty.

With my dad on the line shouting come on, come on, it was perfect when we had the club at the AJY sports day and some of us did rather well ... Then I represented the club at the AJY sports ... That was good because it gave us the opportunity to participate in sports perhaps in a way that we wouldn't have done otherwise. It was a wonderful opportunity to meet other Jewish people in the area of our own age and we were just all great friends.

Interview with male and female club members, 1946–52

WINNING TROPHIES

In its early years, Clapton was not always very successful. With many of its members aged only 12 and the age limit for juniors in AJY competitions set at under 14, its competitors were often at a considerable physical disadvantage, particularly in football. One match ended in a 15–1 defeat. In another, so the story went, to save the team further embarrassment, Lou blew the whistle early when Clapton were losing 18–1!

FOOTBALL
The season in all was literally a washout and very few matches were played. We were entered in the AJY Junior League but

• *Winning trophies … club sports day.*

after two matches Mr Rose thought it advisable that we should be withdrawn. We were so young and small compared with other teams; not that we minded being beaten every match, but enthusiastic as we were, we surely would have lost all our enthusiasm for football had we continued. A series of friendlies were arranged against teams of our own calibre and it proved a good decision as we really enjoyed the matches we played.

We hope that by next season we shall have all put on a little extra weight and are anticipating putting up a good show in the junior league.

Report by male club member, club magazine, April 1947

Indeed, within less than two years, continued involvement in all sporting activities began to produce some very different results, until Clapton became one of the AJY's leading clubs. Year after year it ended as winner and runner-up in almost every competition, achieving more or less full participation in every event.

• *The 1950 football team.*

Its very first success, quite soon after the club started, was in the under 16s division of the AJY's swimming gala. Such was the enthusiasm that a double decker bus was hired to take swimmers, supporters and parents to the event. Imagine the excitement when the club was first and brought home the cup with a team of girls who were just 13. Following this, the club – both boys and girls – enjoyed enormous successes in all age groups.

> **Under the able guidance of Mr Lou Rose this has been an outstanding year of sport. Successes in AJY competitions have included BOYS U'19 CRICKET CUP (for second year), U'16 CROSS COUNTRY RUNNING, U'14 SWIMMING CUP (second year), as well as being second by one point in the U'19 ATHLETICS. The girls were runners up in the U'16 NETBALL COMPETITION, second place in the U'16 ATHLETICS and SWIMMING.**
> *Aid Committee Brochure, 1950*

Other notable achievements included:
- Three C B Fry cup winners (1951 Ronald Brown – 'the highlight of my club days'; 1956 Alan Newton; 1960 Roy Collins). This was presented by the AJY to the outstanding sportsman of the year, not just for sporting success but for sportsmanship, attitudes and character and for general involvement in club life.
- The selection in 1952 of two members (Peter Teitz and Barry Levy) to run for Great Britain in the Maccabiah Games in Israel.
- Alan Rose's representation in 1954 of London's Jewish youth clubs in a boxing tournament against the Brighton Boys' Club. (Tommy Farr, a top boxer at the time, asked Alan, who was rather small, what he

• *Ronald Brown wins C B Fry cup in 1951.*

• *Alan Rose represents the AJY at boxing, 1954.*

was doing up so late and why he wasn't in bed. Even so, Alan brought back the cup.)

In 1958 Clapton, together with the Victoria Boys' Club and with invited guest runners from the Brady Club and clubs in north west London, took part in a transatlantic athletic meeting with the Jewish Community Centre of Canton, Ohio in the USA. An agreed programme of events was held in Canton and in England (at the Finsbury Park running track). In London a panel of judges from Clapton and the AJY officiated and then exchanged the results with the Canton competitors.

CULTURAL ACTIVITIES AND THE WIDER WORLD

In the club I was introduced to some good old unbeatable culture. For the first time in my life I was taking part in discussion groups, debates and drama. These groups did wonders for my self-confidence. I was continually encouraged ... to speak out.

'What my club meant to me', from the AJY magazine, 1957, by male club member, 1946–52

A VISIT TO ANNA LUCASTA

On Monday January 5th, a group of boys and girls from Clapton Club met outside His Majesty's Theatre to see *Anna Lucasta* ... We found it a little difficult to hear what the cast were saying ... Firstly all the cast were negroes and negresses and they spoke with a peculiar accent. Secondly, we were rather high up ... but we soon began to pick up the story. It is rather complicated but most of us understood what it was all about ... When the curtain fell for the last time, we all agreed that we had thoroughly enjoyed ourselves.

Member's report, club magazine, April 1948

One of the things I enjoyed doing most was running the club magazine, *Clapton Confidential* ... I remember the article I wrote in the AJY magazine – 'It couldn't happen here' (about the Holocaust). I wrote a couple of others as well. That again was a good start for writing later on. As you know my career took me into the PR field ...

Interview with male club member, 1950–59

I remember the enchantment of the Moscow State Dance Company and the way we braved a London Pea-souper to get to the West End to see them.

Letter from female club member/manager, 1953–60

CHOICES AND OPPORTUNITIES

In addition to offering its large sporting programme, AJY also ran (for all age groups) a range of other activities and competitions. These included:

- drama festivals;
- arts and crafts festivals;
- music festivals (for individuals and groups);
- fashion shows (a team contest);
- air your views (a team contest);
- quizzes;
- oratory competitions (a team contest); and
- essay competitions.

The AJY also presented a Presidential Award to the year's outstanding member for their character, ability and work in their club. (Clapton member Alan Silver won this in 1966.)

Clapton was active too in a number of national and local competitions and festivals, including:
- exhibiting in art exhibitions organised by Jewish Child's Day;
- Hackney Borough drama festivals;
- London Union of Youth Clubs' drama festivals;
- London Federation of Boys' Clubs general knowledge competition; and
- London Federation of Boys' Clubs chess competition.

These events were very popular, over the years attracting thousands of young people from different clubs and hundreds of leaders and voluntary workers. As with all such competitions, they gave members something to work towards and opportunities to go to other clubs and meet other club members.

The programmes also revealed the quality of the work being done in the clubs which was enabling members to discover talents which sometimes they were encouraged to take further. Two girls from the Clapton club, the Bodlander twins, entered the AJY's music festival during the late '60s when they were 12 years old, singing Hebrew songs from the club's Children's Service choir. They have been entertaining people and giving concerts ever since and are now a sophisticated act with electric guitars. Many others have said that their experience in drama and public speaking competitions enabled them to speak at meetings and on other occasions without being terrified.

TAKING PART – AND WINNING AS WELL

The message is: Value the Club. Do not consider it an organisation you come to on Sunday and Monday to play a game of table tennis and billiards, but an organisation where

each member contributes his or her part and takes out the benefit of knowing that a good job of work has been done.
Letter to the editor, club magazine, April 1947

While Ralph Goldstaub was full-time leader between 1948 and 1951, and indeed through much of the '50s and into the '60s, Clapton took part in all the AJY and the other national associations' inter-club cultural competitions and festivals. At that time there was tremendous enthusiasm for these competitive activities. However, members, with the leaders' encouragement, did not just enjoy them for the sake of 'pot-hunting'. They also found the training and preparation fun and wherever they went they would have an enthusiastic band of supporters. And the competitions opened up opportunities for members to go to other clubs, meet other young people from all parts of London and enjoy the friendships which resulted, both within the club and from outside.

There were many inter-club activities both formal and informal and we made friends and had rivalries with Stamford Hill Club and Hackney Club ... and many others who were members of AJY.
Letter from female club member/manager, 1953–60

Clapton took part in most of these activities and produced many winners and runners-up. For example at one AJY Arts Festival in 1950 Bernard Pincus gained an award for his clay model The Slaying of the Firstborn. The AJY magazine commented that this was a 'most original composition with detail well observed. Figures well placed and expressive. The colour is bold and striking whilst the whole group is pleasing and interesting.' (Bernard became a commercial artist.) Clapton also won the London Federation of Boys' Clubs general knowledge competition in 1951 and for four years running its chess competition – a feat described in the club magazine of 1958 as 'never before accomplished in club history'.

Many of the competitions were memorable – such as the AJY junior drama festivals in the early '50s. These were held at the large East End clubs – Brady, Oxford and St George's, Stepney and West Central – and in some years there were so many groups entered that two sessions were needed. The plays, which had to be on a Jewish theme, could be written by the members – as a number of them were, with a high standard of presentation being the aim and the costumes, usually with the help of parents, being beautifully made. An adjudicator – usually someone well-known – would award gold and silver star certificates to the winners and runners up. There would always be a large audience and the atmosphere was exciting and enjoyable.

Clapton was fortunate that one of its members, Lisa Eppel, was writing and producing plays of an original standard at the age of 13 as well as taking a part in them herself.

Those of us who were fortunate enough to be present at the two sessions of the Drama Festival will have witnessed performances of a high standard. The show must go on, yet just as important is that the actors should enjoy the play for its own sake. It is impossible to comment on the play by the Clapton Junior Club without a special word of praise to Lisa Eppel who wrote The Third Generation, a very moving play depicting so realistically the problem of contemporary Jewish life. It was the story of a family, starting in a concentration camp, then in England and finally in Israel. Indeed the depth of understanding of these problems, to quote the adjudicator, made it difficult at times to realise that the play had been written by one so young. The compliment paid by the adjudicator was that she was so moved that she forgot she was watching a performance by children. 'Here was an instance where each member of the group contributed towards the success and fine achievement of a first class award.'

Review by manager, club magazine, 1951

The AJY fashion shows also proved very popular. Teams were mixed though usually with a predominance of girls. Each one would work on a theme and for a given time would produce its own mini show with a narrator. Judging would be not just on the clothes but also on deportment and overall presentation, with the standard and originality often being very high. The north west clubs took a big part in these competitions which were often held in the north west area.

Vol. 13. No. 2. April 1962.   QUARTERLY 6d.

• *Tony Leifer wins the AJY Chutzpah competition by standing on a platform on Hyde Park corner proclaiming 'ULI ULI IS NIGH'.*

In 1962 the AJY also ran a one-off competition for the Chutzpah Cup, awarded to the member who could get themselves publicity in a national newspaper. Clapton's Tony Leifer won this by standing on a platform in Hyde Park on a

Sunday morning and announcing that a huge plague was on its way to England. Using a huge placard proclaiming 'ULI ULI IS NIGH', he attracted a large crowd and got his photograph in the *Daily Sketch*.

These and many of the other competitions, all still highly competitive, continued until the late '60s, with the fashion shows carrying on into the '70s.

BEYOND COMPETITION

I think the discussion group was so important. We had the feeling that we were trying to influence other people and we were in fact being influenced in a nice way. We were given the opportunity to develop.
Interview with male and female club members, 1946–52

Although many of the activities were part of wider competitions, many were done purely for recreation and fun within the club. On a field nearby members would meet for rounders, cricket and just kicking a football around. In the club billiards, table tennis, chess, draughts and other indoor games were popular while arts and crafts were only occasionally centred around competition. Music and discussion groups were also well supported without any element of competition.

SEX EDUCATION

In the early days of the club, the first leader gave talks to the girls and was considered competent. However, on the evening after the first talk, he was confronted with a most irate mother who strongly objected. She said that she would not have her daughter listen to a talk where words such as penis were used. He decided that perhaps the sessions were not such a good idea after all!

However, a number of years later, in 1956, a certain Claire Rayner was introduced to the club by a manager friend. The club arranged for her to give a series of evening talks in one of the classrooms. After the first talk, so many girls wanted to attend that they queued in the corridor with only the first 40 being allowed in. Claire's talks were an outstanding success and she later did several more series. Little did we know then how well known she was to become.

> **With hindsight ... the talks given us by Claire Rayner when we were 16+ would have been helpful earlier. By the time we were 15/16 we were quite well informed but some social and sexual education when we were 12/13 could have played some part in our attitudes to ourselves and each other ... Growing up in those days seemed a less confident process than it appears today.**
>
> *Letter from female club member/manager, 1953–60*

Unfortunately, we did not have talks for the boys. In those days, it seemed automatic to assume that it was the girls who needed sex education, especially as it was a woman who was directing it.

> **I gave talks for two years (in 1957–58) as I recall. I didn't want to give them only to the girls but I was told very firmly that it was club policy not to mix the sexes for such 'dangerous' material and that their minds were made up and adamant on the issue, so it was no good arguing. So I didn't argue.**

> **But I have a wonderful memory of the very last lecture I gave. I was very pregnant and the girls presented me with this huge bouquet. The girl who gave it to me said (and I can remember every single nuance of what she said): 'This is just to say thank you, and it's not just from us it's from the boys as well who are very grateful.' I did wonder what on earth had been going on though I did know that the girls had been rushing out from my sex information evenings to tell the boys all that they had talked about with me. So I guess maybe I was teaching the boys as well.**

> **The young people were great. They asked intelligent questions, they listened intelligently, they didn't barrack or giggle, and I just remember the whole period as a very jolly one for me. It was virtually my first essay into what might be called public life, as it were, apart from working in hospital. And of course it did prove to be the first step on the way to quite a mixed up career, didn't it? So I shall always remember the Clapton Youth Club with enormous pleasure and satisfaction.**
>
> *Letter from Claire Rayner*

Another course of lectures, again only for girls, was given by the Jewish Marriage Council, in the early '60s. These covered such things as home life, marriage and cooking and just assumed that it was the women who were in charge of the home, especially the cooking.

POLITICS

Mr H. Goodrich MP addressed a large audience at the club premises on Monday evening, January 26th ... (He) told us of the work that went on in the Town Hall, and how important it was that we take an interest in local affairs so that when we are older we could take our places as helpful citizens ... Mr Goodrich then gave an interesting talk on the Houses of Parliament, which was followed by many questions ... and promised to conduct a party over the House during the Easter holidays.
Club magazine, April 1948

... we had various activities but the one which I remember most distinctly now was the discussion group. That was partly because we got into discussing all the ills of the world and how we were going to put it to rights, especially how you can (do that) when you are 14 or 15.
Interview with male and female club members, 1946–52

Though party politics did not have a regular place in the club programme, one unique event took place in 1959, prior to the general election. Three MPs were invited to the club – David Weitzman QC (Labour), Roger White (Conservative) and John Bright (Liberal).

This meeting, an extremely ambitious one, drew a large and appreciative crowd of young people. An extremely lively discussion followed the candidates' speeches, with a large number of intelligent and searching questions. Defence policy, and in particular the possibility of nuclear disarmament, was undoubtedly the centre of interest, but the problems more directly concerning youth, such as education and the status of apprentices and trainees, were also the subject of heated exchange. The interest and active intervention of the audience kept the three candidates continually on their toes.
'Candidates at Clapton Youth Club', Hackney Gazette, 1959

REACHING OUT

As part of the Child's Day activities in May 1947, Pearl Levy gave a talk to members on the Central British Fund and how Jewish young people in Britain could help the children of Europe. The result was that club members decided to set up a committee to 'adopt' a number of the children and provide them with clothing, books and other necessities. A penny a week was collected from all those over 13 with occasionally the proceeds from a dance being added. Every year a donation was made – something which continued throughout the '50s.

We were very proud indeed at a recent Conference of Youth, our club was mentioned as being the one to give a lead in this work, but here we must not sit back on our laurels but must now more than ever redouble our efforts to help the children on the continent. Some good work has been done in collecting clothing, books, chocolate and other useful articles ...
Club magazine, 1948

In 1951 one of the club members, Lorna Greene, was selected to represent British girlhood in the Weston Garfield goodwill tour of Canada. Every year, Weston Garfield, a Canadian biscuit manufacturer, sponsored this trip for 50 girls from all over Britain. They were chosen as 'typically English', representatives for their personality and their ability to be ambassadors from their country. Through the national youth associations clubs were invited to nominate candidates who went before a selection committee. Lorna was given an outfit, cases, accessories and VIP treatment while she was in Canada, including a sightseeing tour.

It was a wonderful wonderful dream come true ... The other day I showed my granddaughter all the pictures. She was quite proud of me!
Interview with Lorna Greene, 1996

SOCIAL DEVELOPMENT AND PERSONAL SUPPORT

THE CLUB AS A SOCIAL CENTRE

... I found myself at home straight away. For the first time I had found a group of friends away from the narrow confines of a school life. I soon began going to the Club regularly ...

'What my club meant to me', from the AJY magazine, 1957, by male Clapton club member/manager, 1946–52

(The club) gave me more space because up to then you only had your own parents to talk to and parents and children have a certain relationship. But here you were able to talk to your own peers, plus the adults ... it was all on a very informal basis as friends. You could expand that way.

Interview with male club member/manager, 1946–68

... in my case I had no other social environment, no other space, no other people with whom I could have an exchange of conversation or anything, except going to the club. I didn't have my room with hi-fis and computers, libraries and places to go and transport. It was a totally different environment.

Interview with male club member, 1946–52

I came to live in the Woodberry Down estate when I was 10 years old. I had lived in Stepney ... Living in a relatively new environment, and on the fourth floor of a block of flats set amongst other blocks, I had no social life ... I must have been 11 or 12 at the time (I joined the club).

Letter from male club member, 1951–57

As I grew up the club became the absolute focus of my life ... My social life and my school life were completely separate ... If the club hadn't existed I not sure what I would have done with my social time ... They were good days even while we were living them.

Interview with male club member, 1950–58

The only nice boy friends I had were boys I knew through the club because they never tried to take advantage of me sexually ...
Interview with female club member, 1962–67

The focal point of the club – its social centre – was the canteen. It was always crowded and had an atmosphere of warmth and friendship. Members of the Parents' Association took responsibility for organising and running it. They would be there from four o'clock so that members could come early, straight from school or, for the older members, from work. They made soup, cooked light meals – eggs, beans on toast – and provided hot and cold drinks, sweets and snacks. Members would come early to chat with friends and games would also be available.

There was a homely feeling attached to the club particularly in the canteen – always too small – with the mothers there regularly helping.
Mick Goldstein, General Secretary, AJY, 1949–81

The parents were very much part of what went on. They would chat with members, getting to know them, creating a family atmosphere. When members went into their groups, some would stay behind to take the opportunity to have a quiet conversation with a manager or leader, sometimes to talk over problems.

At 9.30pm, after assembly (which finished with prayers) and when the group activities were over and members returned from Detmold Road School, everyone would congregate in the canteen. It then got packed and could become quite chaotic – a climax to a well spent evening. Members had the chance to talk to the managers and leaders informally, sharing confidences and experiences, making friendships, enjoying the lively atmosphere. It was a most important part of club life.

The canteen has become a very important institution in the club. The service and management has improved remarkably thanks to the wonderful work put in by Rita Brookman and Martin Compton. At the same time we feel the members should also feel that it is their responsibility in helping to make the sandwiches on Sundays and also in the washing up.
Club magazine, April 1948

The wonder of the new premises ... The big change was the facility for making coffee and chatting. Talking seems to have been a major activity in my life ...
Letter from male club member, 1950–58

With boys and girls mixing socially like this, many romances started at the club at an early age.

We were, I like to feel, great friends, and only toward the end of our time at club did our relationships change from platonic and did we pair up, fairly innocently, as boy and girl friends.
Letter from male club member, 1951–57

Despite much chopping and changing, many of these relationships lasted and resulted in marriage.

We were 14 when we met ... Meeting each other I think was the thing ... a life long partner and that is quite something.
Interview with male and female club members, 1946–52

Many other club friendships have survived over the years and, as the interviews show, people from the different age groups have remained closely linked throughout their lives.

(The club) must have made a great impression. One thing is certain: I have cemented a large number of friendships which have been maintained for over 40 years, apart from marrying (a club member). People I met in those days ... with whom I am still on close social friendly relationships ... no matter how we have all changed, some for better some for worse, it's very much how we knew one another then.
Interview with male club member, 1946–52

HAVING FUN

I think for me home life wasn't very happy and my happiest times were at the club.
Letter from female club member, 1949–55

I must not forget the lighter side of club life. Above all the things I enjoyed most were the countless times we all had a good laugh together ... The social activities extended from dances to Simchas Torah festivities and Purim fancy dress parties. Not only have I had a great deal of fun out of these parties, but I learned ... what is probably the best-known cliché in club language – how to get on with people (also how not to get on with them!).
'What my club meant to me', from the AJY magazine, 1957, by male club member/manager, 1946–52

I was not a great one for socials or dancing although I do remember in the early days we used to go to ballroom dancing lessons down at Detmold Road School and I have to say they have stood me in very good stead ever since. I was taught all sorts of different things I can remember though I never quite mastered the foxtrot. I like to jive a lot, not that I was very dainty at it but I always regretted the fact that that confounded Chubby Checker with his twist put paid to real dancing.

Interview with male club member, 1950–59

The New Year's Eve dance. Staying at the club until midnight. Looking at my watch to see how much time we had left. Decorating the club for those evenings. The themes we devised ... the coffee lounge becoming the *Green Door*, which was a Frankie Vaughan hit.

Letter from male club member, 1951–57

I can remember running dances at the club, Helen Shapiro singing to us ... She was always going to make it as a singer ... She used to sing at the club at the socials, if we had a dance going on she would sing – she didn't specifically come to sing, she was just a kid at the club who had a good voice.

Interview with male club member/manager, 1952–66

It was a place of happy events and everyone was on an equal footing ... Laughter and happy faces stick in my mind.

Letter from female club member/manager 1949–57

We weren't forced to do anything ... it was a contrast from school (where) you had a curriculum (and) you had to do things this way. There were of course limitations in the club but you were pretty well free to develop, to interact with other people. At school you tend to be very self centred. It's just you and the exam at the end of the road and you are competing. But it was give and take in the club. You met them (other club members) as colleagues, on an equal footing.

Interview with male and female club members, 1946–52

ORGANISING DANCES

The social committee was very well organised and a very important part of the club. They were in charge of the club socials and planned and organised the dances, taking complete responsibility. As we have seen,

• *Jiving the Clapton way – dressed in our best clothes.*

there were always special dances to celebrate Chanukah (the Festival of Lights), Purim (the story of Esther) and Simchath Torah (the Rejoicing of the Law). A big dance was always arranged for New Year's Eve and for Valentine's Day, with the club decorated in the theme of the latest hit song – for example, The Green Door or Fernando's Hideaway.

The club would buzz with anticipation for these occasions and the members would dress up in their best clothes – at one period the girls wearing full printed skirts with lots of underskirts, very feminine and pretty, and the boys in their best trousers and jackets.

On one occasion, in 1960, a big dance was being arranged about six months ahead. When the club social committee members were considering bands, one of them said he'd heard of a very good group in Liverpool who wanted £50 to play. We would also have to give them a contract. After some discussion, the committee decided it was too much to pay. Just six months later, at the time that the dance was to take place, the Beatles hit the national and international headlines!

CARING FOR INDIVIDUALS

Henry Koor was there in 1947 when my father died. I remember he took me to one side in one of the rooms and had a long talk

to me about coping. I've never forgotten that ...
Interview with male club member, 1946–55

... without realising it at the time many of the people who managed, helped, led the club ... had a far greater knowledge and understanding and feeling for us than we ever, ever knew, realised or appreciated at the time. Years later we understood it.
Interview with male club member, 1946–52

(As a committee member) I also found how comprehensive is the range of duties of leaders, managers and other persons with responsible positions in the club. I saw how they deal with personal problems – some so delicate that the boy or girl concerned went to their club leader rather than to their own parents.
'What my club meant to me', from the AJY magazine, 1957, by male club member/manager, 1946–52

As I grew into teenage years, the club leaders ... meant everything to me. I was a very difficult child at home ... My parents had not had the advantage of prolonged education or success in commerce. They were unreligious, taking no part in communal structures. They were at a loss to cope with my aspirations for education, career and a modicum of affluence which seemed then absolutely unattainable.

Going to the club each week, having so many friends of both sexes, learning about Judaism from my peers in the main, attending Shabbath morning services, helped to alleviate the frustrations of my existence. Being able to lose oneself in so much activity, social and educational was the healthiest option open to me ...
Letter from female club member/manager, 1953–60

Leaders and managers at Clapton supported many individual members when they were in difficulties, usually behind the scenes without anyone – even other adults in the club – knowing. Two situations known to me illustrate this – though all the names and some of the details have been changed.

Joan

Joan was 12 when she joined as one of the club's founder members in 1946. She was a gentle quiet girl, always helpful, who took part in cultural activities like drama, discussion groups and essay competitions.

She did not mix very well with other members but seemed happy in the club. An only child, she was born late in the lives of her parents who doted on her – her mother particularly was very possessive. Her father was a tailor by profession.

Joan formed an attachment to one of the managers, Ruth, which developed into a very deep affection. Ruth, a manager, had not had this kind of involvement with a member before nor had she had any training for dealing with the situation. She tried to take it in her stride, not treating Joan any differently from other members. However, she was aware of Joan's strong feelings for her and that, as Joan seemed to believe that her parents did not understand her, she was coming to see Ruth as something of a mother figure. However, there was never any physical contact between them.

Joan's parents had great hopes for her, wanting her to stay at school and go to university. But she left school at 16 and went to a commercial college to do shorthand and typing. Though she did very well there and reached an extremely high standard, her choice caused disagreements at home. Though Ruth tried to get Joan's parents to see Joan's point of view, Joan could not cope with their high expectations for her and the pressure they were putting on her and she became depressed.

One evening in the club, she told Ruth she had taken a large dose of aspirin. On another occasion she called Ruth to her home after doing the same thing. Her parents were distraught – they said she was doing this quite often and they could not understand why – she was being very difficult. By now she was attending the doctor.

This pattern continued for about a year, with many ups and downs. Ruth always tried to be there for her, and also kept in close touch with her parents. Then Joan had a breakdown. She was admitted to a psychiatric hospital and kept in for several months. Ruth went to see her regularly, something the hospital encouraged. Though Joan talked very little, Ruth found that she only wanted to see her, not her parents.

After a few months of treatment, the hospital said Joan could go home for a weekend. When this was put to her, she said she did not want to go to her parents but to Ruth's home. (Ruth was married and had three older children.) In consultation with the doctor it was arranged that, if Ruth was willing, Joan's first outing could be to her, for an afternoon visit. At this stage, expert advice and support was found for Ruth through the AJY.

When the visit took place, Ruth's family left her alone for some time with Joan who particularly talked to her about going home. Ruth recalls

Joan standing at the window looking out into a beautiful sunset and saying: 'This is my home, this is where I belong.' However, when Ruth took her back to the hospital, she seemed happy and relaxed.

After that, Joan did visit her own home and eventually was discharged and came back to the club. Two or three years later, she brought a young man to the club to whom, much to Ruth's delight she had transferred her affection. They became engaged and had a big wedding at which Ruth was very much honoured, especially by Joan's parents.

The young couple set up home quite close to Clapton. Joan's parents suggested that Ruth visited them in their own home but Ruth decided that if they wanted to get in touch with her, Joan knew where to contact her. She never did, suggesting that by then she wanted to put her past behind her. Several years later we heard secondhand that Joan had again been depressed.

Kate

Kate joined the club at the age of 14. She was never a popular member – she was often very rude, swore a lot and did not fit in with the other girls of her age who were rather 'nice'. Though they firmly rejected her, she continued to come to the club regularly. She tried hard to be friends with a particular group though they too were not very warm towards her.

Kate formed an attachment to one of the managers, Esther, which gradually developed into a dependency. Esther talked to the group, hoping to get them to understand that Kate was lonely. She also talked to Kate, trying (unsuccessfully) to get her to calm her ways. The girls just did not like her and the more they showed it the more aggressive Kate became, even getting into fights.

Esther managed to get one girl to befriend Kate, which seemed a good idea at the time. However, it resulted in both girls being shut out. Kate's attachment to Esther then increased: the club was on the top floor, and when Esther arrived, she would look up to see Kate standing by the window looking out for her. The more Kate was rejected at the club, the more she clung to Esther and the more Esther's efforts to win over the other members failed.

Though Esther managed to get Kate to take part in some of the groups, she was battling all the way as Kate became increasingly difficult. Esther felt that the situation was getting out of hand – it was by now worrying her a great deal. The club leader at the time was also very helpful, getting to know Kate well and working to get her accepted in the club. He and

Esther discussed the situation at great length. Esther also sought some expert advice from outside the club, including sending recordings of how she was feeling to an experienced youth worker for comment, and gradually began to feel more confident about her work with Kate.

Kate was an only child and was obviously unhappy. When she said she did not get on with her parents, Esther offered to meet them. Kate did not want that – she just wanted Esther. Esther never did fully understand the situation with the parents – in fact she never got to meet them as she felt she could not go against Kate's wishes. However, Kate stayed at the club for about three years, eventually settling down a little better. Though the girls never fully accepted her, after a while she became a little less aggressive and they were a little more friendly towards her.

THE MISSED ONES?

When I reached 15 years ... my parents decided that I should leave grammar school and get a job. I was so ashamed that I barely spoke of it to anyone. Reflecting now, I know I should have asked for help ... but I didn't.
Letter from female club member, 1953–60

I remember the concerts with Connie Brill, the netball, athletics and swimming. All the good things – I seemed to do most things in those days and that's good.

I left the club when I was about 15 – too soon. Why I left I cannot tell you. Anything which was good and where we were admired for ourselves, we ran away from, and I think that is something that if the club had been around today you might have spotted, and perhaps tried to seek me out and find out why I left. I can't remember the circumstances and what reasons I gave, but I know I have never found anything like it again.

I don't know if the club influenced my later life because there was always that shadow there, and well I don't quite know what to say about that.
Interview with female club member, 1946–51

While we may hold on to a picture of everyone socialising and being happy in the club, many members who might have been helped and advised were probably missed. (Some, for example, left the club early without anyone finding out why.) Even with (sometimes two) full-time leaders in post, the membership became too large for them to pick up all the members' personal problems. This work would therefore often be left to the managers.

For some young people a manager would anyway have been the most appropriate helper. Nonetheless, though managers received some training and would confer with the leader and even seek further advice, this was not always sufficient to allow them to spot all the problems or to cope with many of the individual difficulties members faced. Indeed, it is doubtful whether there was as much concentration in the club on the social and the personal aspects of members' lives as was needed.

THE CLUB AWAY FROM HOME

AWAY FOR THE DAY

• *Summer outing to Whipsnade.*

As holidays were rare at the time the club started, to go for a day out was a treat. Rambles were popular – to Epping Forest or Box Hill in Surrey – with the ones for juniors always being led by a manager. Outings by coach were made to Thaxted, Whipsnade and other places of interest. Sometimes there were separate outings for boys and girls.

• *Day trip round London.*

One Sunday January 22nd a merry party set off by bus to Whipsnade with Mr Koor and Mr and Mrs Rose. It was the first time many of us had been there and it was ... most enjoyable to spend a day walking round

the pleasant fields and seeing all the animals in their natural surroundings ... Many of our party enjoyed the novelty of elephant and camel rides, while groups picnicked in the fields which overlook Dunstable Downs. We sang lustily all the way home ...

Club magazine, April 1948

Trips to the seaside were also a particular treat, especially when they involved Lew Greene. Lew, a parent, was a haulage contractor who owned a large lorry to carry furniture. To make it more comfortable for passengers he would put four mattresses from his home in the back and then take about twenty boys and girls for Sunday day trips to Shoeburryness!

HOLIDAYS AT HOME

I came to the club because I was invited to go to a club holiday ... I loved it, absolutely. It was the first time I'd been away from my parents – the first time I'd mixed outside my home with another group of people – and it was just wonderful.

Interview with male club member, 1951–59

I went away to my first inter club weekend at Brady Club's Skeet House in (the) winter ... and have never forgotten how remote the house seemed, the long walks, the pyjama party, heaven for a kid from my background.

Letter from female club member/manager, 1953–60

Club holidays were fun – for socialising and adventure. They were also inexpensive, with one every year for a number of years to Bracklesham Bay and also other places such as the Brady Club's Skeet House. Members clearly have nostalgic memories of them, especially recalling the sing-songs and making their entertainment.

LEIGH HOUSE, BRACKLESHAM BAY

In 1943 a memorial fund was set up in the name of Sir Max Bonn as a tribute to his services to Jewish and non-Jewish young people. Its object was to acquire a suitable house to be used as a centre for the clubs and

• *View of Leigh House.*

Jewish Lads' Brigade units affiliated to the AJY. Mr M. Kennedy Leigh offered his house at Bracklesham Bay near Chichester in Sussex. Though it had been requisitioned by the military during the war and was in a bad state of repair, it was a beautiful house which had a garden which led straight onto the beach. In 1946 it was adapted to accommodate 15 young people and in 1947 named the Sir Max Bonn Youth Centre, Leigh House. Later it was extended to accommodate 35. After conversion, as well as the dormitories, it had a games room, showers and good catering facilities. The architect for this work was the well known and dedicated youth worker Ernest M. Joseph. (This information was taken from Charles Magnus's *E.M. Joseph: The Man and his Work*.)

During the summer, clubs would book a week's holiday there (I believe Clapton was the first club to do this) and during the winter it would be used for training and conferences. From 1949 a regular Clapton club holiday was held there every summer until 1963. The first three holidays were for girls only, after which the club took mixed groups.

As this was immediately after the war and the members were not used to having holidays, this for them was a luxury. They made their own entertainment, with swimming at any time an added bonus. The resident wardens at that time, the Welbys, were very popular and good friends to all the clubs.

... the trips to Bracklesham Bay ... I was a fairly shy individual and eventually I decided to go ... I must say that I enjoyed that weekend enormously. They were exciting times and we had a speaker along who touched on a fairly racy subject like the

• *Bracklesham Bay, 1952.*

McCarthy witch hunts in America at that time which we all took terribly to heart. He was obviously incensed about what was going on there and managed to incense us as well.
Interview with male club member, 1950–59

I visited Bracklesham Bay twice ... I think it must have been the first time that I had ever been on holiday for a whole week ... These holidays were magic: they widened my circle of friends at the club, so that club members that once I would have been too shy to talk to became rather special ... It was at Bracklesham ... that (my first girl friend) and I became what is

• *Bracklesham Bay, 1950 fancy dress party.*

now known as an 'item'. We started flirting on the coach before we started ... and I remember holding hands with her while in the sun lounge in the house ...

Letter from male club member, 1951–57

... the back of the house was magical. It stood before a lawn which led through a gate to a shingled beach over which, it seemed, we exercised sole rights ... At night we sat and listened to the waves and counted the suicidal moths attracted to our lights ...

As we grew older supposedly surreptitious challenges to the night time segregation were devised. Poor Uncle Lou maintained vigil on the stairs, at the windows and drainpipes. It was of course like trying to stem the tide. The boys sneaked in by one means or another and joined their girlfriends for fairly innocent goings on.

Letter from female club member/manager, 1953–60

CAMPS AND OTHER ADVENTURES

Although most of the clubs at that time had a long history of camping holidays, the Clapton club did not camp every year. It did use the AJY camp at Stapleford Abbots and one year some of the boys joined the Victoria Club at their camp on the Isle of Wight.

• *Boys' camping holiday to the Isle of Wight, 1947.*

• *On the way to Bexhill …*

However, Ralph Goldstaub was always an adventurous leader and the holidays he arranged certainly were that. He rented boarding schools – at Bexhill, in Devon and Cornwall and at Frinton – and with the help of parents, particularly Charlie Abrahams (by then club chairman) and his wife Twink, arranged that all crockery and utensils conformed with kashrut (the Jewish religious observance) and did all the cooking.

I remember the holidays. First of all that too was a new generation, the idea of club outings of the old clubs was that you … pitch your tent in a field and eat outdoors. I started out with the idea that a certain amount of sophistication and luxury was in order so we rented a boarding school for holidays where they had a sports field and a swimming pool and facilities that normally clubs don't have.

We also made very good use of Leigh House and had a number of very exciting weekends where the youngsters learned how to do something, talk about something and form relationships – and be kept apart!

… Some of the weekends were training weekends and some of them were more adventurous. Many of them were training, concentrating on some subject to discuss and learn about, but my goal was to give a foretaste of college – to be together … learn how to relate to each other, to form friendships based on social contacts. Sometimes it needed me sitting on the stairs between the two groups at 11 or 12 o'clock at night, but basically they learned what is appropriate and what is not appropriate …

Interview with Ralph Goldstaub, club leader, 1948–51

GOING ABROAD

Israel

... the Israel trip remains as a high spot in my memory. That clearly was a very significant part of my life. (It was) the first time I had been abroad ... (and indeed thanks to you and Lou that I did it because) my parents certainly couldn't afford the money at the time. The Jewish Agency made concessionary rates for all the members, enabling us to go.

Interview with male club member, 1950–59

- *'The Israel trip remains a high spot in my memory.'*

In 1958 the Jewish Agency sponsored a trip to Israel for the Clapton Club – 24 members went. An attached outside group of 12 also soon became part of the Clapton party, with ages ranging from 16 to 21. Lou and I lead the trip after spending a year preparing for it. This included providing instruction on the history of Israel and lessons in the Hebrew language and in Israeli singing and dancing. There was great excitement in the build up to the holiday.

> **The … year was taken up saving (£2 weekly paid in at the club), group discussions and many educational projects. We learned about Zionism and Jewish history, subjects which had been neglected in my education … We younger members of the group benefited greatly from the age range which was 16 to 20+. We were able to learn so much from people who were now in further education and were most knowledgeable about religion.**
> *Letter from female club member/manager, 1953–60*

We were away six weeks – one week's journey each way and four weeks actually in Israel. The journey was long – from the moment the parents waved us off at the club via a coach to Victoria Station, train to Folkstone, the channel crossing to Bologne, a stop in Paris and then to Marseilles. Though the trains were hot and crowded, wherever we stopped the members managed to find a space and the energy to dance and sing.

At Marseilles, we boarded the Artza which, though only the size of a Channel steamer, had 400 people on board. They were all emigrants and youth groups, for whom the boat had been adapted with dormitories sleeping 40. However, because the nights were very warm, many of the passengers slept on deck – though, with the singing and dancing going on until the early hours, no-one seemed to need much sleep. After five days on board, the landing at Haifa brought great emotion and excitement.

We were joined with a group from the Stamford Hill Club and travelled the country in two coaches, each with two very capable young guides. The Jewish Agency had planned a very full and arduous itinerary which involved travelling the length and breadth of Israel and stopping at and touring all the places of interest right down to Eilat. It was very hot and very exhausting (some members of course managed to disappear whenever there were very tiring walking tours!).

The accommodation was varied – mainly youth hostels and students hostels. In Eilat there was nowhere to stay as nothing had been built there yet. So we slept on the beach and had breakfast (covered with flies) on long trestle tables. We also stayed a week at a Kibbutz – where we had to work four hours a day. Though this did not seem too hard, working in the intense heat in the fields picking apples and in the kitchen gave us some idea of what life in Israel was like. We mixed with the young people, spent the long hot evenings in discussions and just enjoyed the atmosphere. In all the trip was both educational and great fun – an experience of a lifetime crammed into six weeks.

When we returned the 'Israel group' met regularly for Saturday afternoon teas and many functions designed to maintain contact with members of the group who joined our Clapton nucleus from other areas of London. Friendships (which are) retained to this day.
Letter from female club member/manager, 1953–60

SWEDEN

As a result of his visit to Scandanavia in 1957, Jeffrey Leifer suggested that the AJY organise an AJY party for a visit to Sweden. This took place in l959, led by Michael Harris. Michael, then a manager at the North West Boys' Club, was later to become one of the most active workers at the AJY and its chairman between 1990 and 1994.

• *Members of the group in Sweden.*

At that time, the Scandinavian Jewish Youth Federation held a congress and camp each year in one of the main cities of Norway, Sweden, Denmark or Finland. In 1959 it was the turn of the Swedish capital, Stockholm, to host this. As a part of the AJY's Diamond Jubilee celebrations a group of club members were chosen to be the first-ever delegation from the AJY to go to Scandinavia – 7 of the 11 members were from Clapton.

They spent a weekend in Stockholm, met the other Scandinavian campers and travelled together to Lillsved, 27 miles away. Then followed seven days of discussions, swimming, dancing and generally having a very good time. They then returned to Stockholm for the Congress attended by representatives of all four of the Scandinavian countries. On the way home they also spent a day in Amsterdam.

HOLIDAYS ABROAD

In later years club leaders met the demands of young people who were moving with the times. In the late '60s, Leon Rogers joined with the Stamford Hill and Victoria Clubs to take 150 members on holiday to Belgium while the groups which Jack and Rose Langham took to Italy stayed in commercial hotels. Times were certainly changing.

PART THREE

ENDINGS
AND REFLECTIONS

We hear people criticising and condemning today's young people, reminiscing of days gone-by, sadly shaking their heads. "The youth aren't what they used to be". Are we so bad? It occurred to me that at this special time, our Diamond Jubilee, it would be a good idea to seek the opinions of people with a wealth of experience in youth work.

I was privileged to visit three pioneers of the Girls' Club movement. Unfortunately, Lady Henriques, who I also wished to visit, was in hospital—I do hope she is well now.

NO FUTURE FOR THE CLUBS

The Hon. Lily Montagu, founder of the West Central Girls' Club felt that Club leaders have a more difficult task today. In former years girls who lived in poor conditions and had few advantages depended on the club. They were responsive to affection and sympathy. Today the problem is quite different. Girls have so much material comfort at home that they don't need the club so much. However, the modern girl still needs sympathy and understanding. As for interests, the clubs must now offer not ordinary activities, but novelties and new ideas.

I asked Miss Montagu if she thought that youth today was as black as it is painted; she replied that youth is not black at all but there is too much pampering by adults. Hooliganism is an outlet; young people need their energies directed into the right channels. With regard to behaviour and religious outlook the home influence is vital. In clubs, young people don't like "to be done good to", and club leaders need a special approach. Self-management in the club is most important, and a mixture of age-groups healthy. Mixed clubs are now essential, although there must be adequate provision for separate interests.

As a Minister of religion, Miss Montagu is convinced that all clubs must have a religious basis. Unfortunately, she does not think that there is a future for clubs; study groups for further education and

Miss Moses agreed that ... young people today are more restless, less club conscious and not so satisfied in their club life ...

The Hon Lily Montagu, founder of the West Central Girls' Club, felt that club leaders have a more difficult task today. In former years girls who lived in poor conditions and had few advantages depended on the club ... Today girls have so much material comfort at home that they don't need the club so much ... As for interests, the clubs must now offer not ordinary activities, but novelties and new ideas ... Unfortunately, she does not think there is a future for clubs.

'All about Eve' by a Clapton member, from the AJY magazine,
Jewish Youth, *1959*

LIFE AFTER CLAPTON

THE CLAPTONIANS

In 1951 Charlie Abrahams became club chairman. He was an ex-Oxford and St George's member who brought all the ideals and training of his old club days with him to Clapton. He and his wife Twink, with her musical ability at the piano and sparkling personality, made a great contribution to the club and to the Parents' Association.

At about the time Charlie took over, the club's first members were reaching 18. As we have seen, several of them became managers and some went to other clubs as helpers and to get further experience while many of the boys did National Service. Even so, the Club Committee decided to start a section for the over 18s. Charlie called a meeting at his house to launch The Claptonians. It was agreed they should have an evening to themselves and be completely self-supporting. They started in 1951 with 32 members.

For a few years they survived. They met socially on a Thursday evening and carried on with the same kinds of sporting activities as before. However, as several married at an early age (20) and many of the boys went to do their National Service, numbers began to fall. Yogi Mayer, director of the Brady Boys' Club and at that time a leading youth worker in the Jewish community, counselled against trying to hold on to them. 'Encourage them to find other interests outside the club,' he advised. 'After all, that's what a club should train them for.' The Claptonians closed – though, by helping to produce a number of good young managers, it was not a total failure.

OLD GIRLS AND BOYS

In 1957 some of the Claptonians who were still meeting socially formed a committee to run a money-raising dinner and ball for the club. It was a black tie occasion held at the Selby's Banqueting Hall in the West End, was well supported by ex-members and parents and was most successful both socially and financially.

• *Celia and Lou Rose at the Claptonians' First Dinner and Ball.*

By 1960 this group had disbanded. However, some of them who had remained in touch with the club felt that, following the 1957 experience, they would like to re-create the group and arrange further fundraising functions, although many were now married, and living out of the district.

But at the meeting they called there was no enthusiasm to get together again or to be involved in fundraising. Although those of us still involved in the club were disappointed, one of the ex-members, in summing up the situation, clearly echoed Yogi Mayer's earlier view: 'What would you rather have, a group of old members meeting for nostalgic memories, or a group of mature people actively involving themselves in their local communities?'

Again in the early '60s a small group of founder members who had kept in close touch with Lou and I asked us to meet with them because they were again considering making an attempt to raise money for the club. They felt that many of the ex-members were now so well established, many as professionals and in business, that now was the time! They were sure that there would be great enthusiasm for a big function and they would have no difficulty selling tickets. It was agreed to book a large hall and a good band, and to put down a deposit of £200. Sadly not many tickets were sold and five couples were out of pocket to cover the loss to the tune of £40 – not a small sum at the time.

In 1967, while he was the club's full-time leader, Leon Rogers tried again to start a senior club, once more without success. His epitaph was telling:

I think a great deal of good came from the experiment – contact is maintained with the old members. But they manage to survive without the club.
Leon Rogers, club leader 1965–68, in the club magazine

For many years, there were no regular reunions of Clapton members – as there were for several other of the larger London Jewish clubs. Members did meet together in their various age groups on many occasions and large reunions were eventually held in 1986 and 1989 and again in 1996. Parties have also been organised for Ralph Goldstaub when he has visited Britain from America where he has now lived for many years.

However, the Claptonians' experience suggests that there has been no place and certainly no necessity to set up a club for adults in Clapton.

A CHANGING COMMUNITY, A DECLINING CLUB

A NEW GENERATION

Miss Gerson does not think that the young people today are any different; they have the misfortune of living in a financially easier time, of having more indulgent parents, and they thus lack initiative and leadership.
'All about Eve' by a Clapton member, from the AJY magazine, Jewish Youth, *1959*

By the late '50s and early '60s, the youth scene was changing. Young people were getting more ambitious. More school activities were on offer and, as their earnings grew, members could afford to frequent the growing number of discos and could follow up other interests outside the club. Though drinking was never a major factor for this generation, it was also becoming fashionable to meet and socialise in pubs. Social life therefore was no longer centred entirely around the club.

The employment scene was also changing. For a large number of the boys, taxi-driving was increasingly attractive – a trend which has continued to this day – and it seemed too that very few girls were going on to university. However, the girls were by now getting more skilled in secretarial, hairdressing and work in stores, and were taking on other kinds of training. Even after marriage, most of them continued to work until they had children. When their children went to school they often then developed new skills and took up new careers.

At this time too, as we have seen, the number of Jewish families leaving Clapton gradually increased. Though many had to start modestly in rented accommodation within the area until they saved up enough to buy a house, this was the generation which steadily moved out into Essex and to north west London.

FROM DECLINE TO CLOSURE

We started to see the waiting list diminish, the interest in youth clubs falling off as coffee shops in the West End were beginning to take people's interest. Rather than come to a dance on a Saturday night they'd go to the West End and sit around drinking expresso coffee – the expresso machines had just arrived ... I remember saying we had to buy a television and they were saying you shouldn't buy a television – if they want to watch TV they can stay at home.
Interview with male club member/manager, 1949–57

All this led to an inevitable fall from the mid '60s in the club's membership. In 1960 the membership was 350, with members taking part in almost everything the AJY and the other national youth organisations had to offer. Their experience in the club was giving them confidence, they were taking part in many competitions and activities which were new to them, and they were visiting other clubs.

From 1961 to 1964 the club had no full-time leader. Joan and Leon Pratt were appointed part-time leaders for the Junior Club but the main club relied on a group of managers and a number of senior members who had trained in the club. Though the council and committee structure continued and some of the parents were still involved, particularly in the running of the canteen, this group of young people spent all their time and energy at the club. They took complete responsibility, dealing competently with all aspects of the work involved – a quite amazing achievement.

It was at that point, 1965, that Leon Rogers was appointed full-time leader. He was one of the first products of the 1960 *Albemarle Report* on the youth service and of the National College for the Training of Youth Leaders in Leicester which resulted from it. A number of the senior members and managers stayed together with a small number of the original loyal parents, with some newer members becoming involved. According to one of Leon's reports in the club magazine, it was impressive to find a club so well and so democratically run by this small group of volunteers.

However, with the families moving away and with the needs of the members changing, by 1965 the membership continued to decrease steadily. Jack Langham, an LCC table tennis coach, continued to run the club between 1968 and 1973 as a part-time leader. In 1973 the decision was taken that there were no longer enough young people to warrant keeping the club open.

In 1974, the Highbury and Dalston Club were without premises because their synagogue was closing. Harold Marco, the leader, moved into the Clapton premises, re-opening the club as Clapton and Highbury. It continued in a small way for about four more years.

THE CLAPTON EFFECT

THE IMPACT OF THE CLUB

Even though it would be wrong to suggest these successes were the direct result of being a Clapton member, many of the members themselves, in interviews and letters, make their own statements about the impact of the Clapton club on them – and on aspects of their lives which include but also go well beyond their careers.

Developing talents and shaping careers

> **(In) my career today, if I've had any success it's because I was given an arena in which to operate ... I was given the opportunity to take the reins, to lead people, to organise people.**
> *Interview with male club member/manager, 1949–57*

> **I was involved in the social side of the club running dances on a Sunday eventually culminating in a very ambitious dance to raise money at Brady Girls' Club ... It was quite ambitious because – I must have been about 15 – I saw Van Stratton and his band ... At that time Van Stratton at the Brady Club was like bringing in Elton John, a hit name ...The thing was a total sell-out. It gave me confidence that I could work out expenses, work out an exercise of business ... Though it was nothing to do with business, in a vague form it made me realise that maybe I had the commercial ability.**
> *Interview with male club member, 1946–55*

> **It gave me some confidence because I'm by nature a very shy person ... People were very friendly – that made me realise that once you put your foot over the threshold people will welcome you. After the club I did a drama course and there I met my husband ... I don't think I would have gone to the drama course if I hadn't gone to the club.**
> *Interview with Norma Yellin, drama instructor, 1955–57*

> **Some highlights for me are to do with my own personal development. I got very involved through the club with drama**

and public speaking ... Things I was enabled to do through the club have formed what my whole life has been about – not only my interests but my career.

Interview with female member/manager, 1953–60

Getting a sense of community ...

The Clapton club was my avenue into a new world. Its strength lay in the way it was embedded in its neighbourhood. Kids joined from within a large radius. The club influenced my life at that vulnerable time when you have to learn how to grow up and find examples to learn from. At Clapton I found those examples and experiences. I will always be grateful that the club was there and drew in so many good people who gave freely to create such an environment.

Letter from female club member/manager, 1953–60

A club makes you feel part of a community, and if you have got the right influence then you care about other people, you learn to care about others because you are not just you, you are part of the team. We used to support the football, we supported the cricket, we played netball, we had our supporters, we were part of the team, we felt part of Clapton.

Interview with female club member/manager, 1949–56

The club definitely influenced my teenage years, definitely a big influence on my life. Definitely a sense of belonging, it made you feel secure when you were there. It was like a second home to me. It enabled me to do things and go places that we would never have gone to, like the holiday in Sweden.

Interview with female club member, 1950–59

... within a Jewish ethos

It was a Jewish club for Jewish families and their children ... It was culturally rich both at the spiritual level and the wider area of culture ... a focus for teenagers to get together and to do things cooperatively and independently ... I gained a lot out of it in terms of friendship and companionship and growing up together.

Interview with male club member, 1951–59

In particular I remember when Greville Janner came to

adjudicate one of the speech competitions. The particular topic was how Judaism can be a link in a chain and (how) we go forward from one generation to another in that way by being links in a chain. He made a reference to the fact that that was exactly what was happening here at this club ... On that particular day it was like it brought to a head for me the fact that ... here was I winning a speech competition by speaking about being a link in a chain ... and feeling ... I was living it through being part of this community. It was one of those red letter days when you suddenly find everything comes together ... (When I) question what my roots are about, where they come from, every time ... it comes back to Clapton. So much that I experienced there has led me through my life to be what I am.

Interview with female club leader and club member, 1950–55

Learning to meet and get on with people

One of Somerset Maugham's sayings sums up my feelings about the club generally – he said that from every person one meets in a lifetime a little is gained and retained for one's own personal use. It is that gain, that retention, that for me has made Clapton really worthwhile ...

'What my club meant to me', from the AJY magazine, 1957, by club male member/manager, 1946–52

The club had a great influence on my teenage years – it was somewhere I could readily mix with my friends – enjoy sport – meet girls and generally enjoy my social hours.

Letter from male club member/manager, 1957–68

The club influenced my life immeasurably. It gave me confidence to meet people, especially girls, and prepared me for social life at university ... Clapton may appear to have provided its club members with too little responsibility and breadth of experience. However, I think it important to recognise that the conditions of children now and then are very different. We had little money ... We didn't have the experience of travel. In short, we didn't have the confidence of today's youth ... The AJY scene of the '50s served the needs of a mainly working-class community. So far as I am concerned, it did its job well for us at that time.

Letter from club member, 1951–57

• *The club had a great influence on my teenage years – it was somewhere I could readily mix with my friends – enjoy sport – meet girls and generally enjoy my social hours.'*

It taught you how to mix with people ... I'll never forget the camaraderie and the friendship ...
Interview with male club member, 1946–55

I made very good friends who I still keep in touch with today from the club years.
Interview with female club member, 1950–59

Making – and keeping – friends

... my greatest friendships in life were formed at that club.
Interview with female club member/manager, 1955–58

... the majority of our friends are all ex-club members ... (In) my teenage years ... all my friends were from the club.
Interview with male and female club members, 1946–53

All my friends were there and I'm still in touch with them – I see friends from the club to this day.
Interview with male club member/manager, 1952–66

The club certainly influenced ... my friendships ... We get together on simchas and other times – I'm very close to those people.
Interview with female club member, 1962–67

Touching lives – and principles

The club certainly influenced my principles that I still have today.
Interview with female club member, 1962–67

When I did actually go out a bit, which wasn't until I was about 20 or 21, I found it quite difficult ... But later on in life I realised that very solid beginnings stand you in tremendous good stead for everything else that happens ... (It was) a small sheltered bonded community perhaps without a tremendous amount going on outside of itself and yet quite a lot of involvement really ... with other clubs, going on holidays, things I would never have done in any other way. (It was) a chance to experience a community that cared in a way that would allow you to go on and experience other things if you chose to ... So it's almost like a reversal of saying there were limitations ... that closeness, that community, enables one throughout life to go on and explore fearlessly ...

Interview with female club member, 1950–55

It did mean a lot to me, I think perhaps more now than it did then. We didn't realise then ... it was club, it was perhaps taken for granted.

Interview with female club member, 1950–59

When I look back, I think Clapton was a quite remarkable institution, and in retrospect had a great influence on the course of my life.

Letter from Norman Spector, manager, 1956–63

Having fun – and a social life

If you ask for my memories, it would be the socials and sporting events, the happy memories.

Interview with male club member, 1946–52

I look back on it as a very formative part of my life – something I enjoyed enormously. I was there continuously from 15 to 18 ... I used to come every night. It certainly did my O level results no good at all but I took the lesson for my A level. It was too attractive and I was addicted to it at the expense of my academic studies.

Interview with male club member, 1950–59

I didn't know any other social life – basically that was it ... All my friends were there ... I still see friends from the club to this day ... (It was a) total family club ... a family atmosphere.

Interview with male club member/manager, 1952–66

... we lived to go to the club – that was our life, we didn't know any other life.
Interview with female club member, 1946–55

The club <u>was</u> my teenage years ...
Letter from male club member, 1951–57

WITH THE WISDOM OF HINDSIGHT

Though Clapton had professional leaders for most of the time, many of us involved with the club were not trained – especially the people who were originally involved and helped set it up. We were only one generation away from the members, and one generation away from the immigrants who, like so many East End Jews, had fought their way out of poverty. Certainly we did not have the advantages or the education of the pioneers of the Jewish youth movement which began at the turn of the century. Some of their families had been in Britain for generations and were regarded as kings and queens in their large settlement clubs. They dominated the youth work of their era.

Since 1939 (when youth work was given an educational slant) there are many club leaders who would regard themselves in the same category as headmaster or mistress of a school, and who regard their assistants as teacher-helpers rather than solely helpers or social workers. There was a fair amount of authoritarianism, a concept of social betterment, of 'doing good to' rather than 'with'.
J. Macalister Brew, Youth and Youth Groups

What Macalister Brew says was true of the Jewish pioneers. In the early years the clubs they set up had been in deprived areas where there was poverty and the children were in need of food and clothing. The leader's role was to help the poor – to keep the boys and girls off the streets, to prevent juvenile delinquency. These men and women of private means came into the areas and gave their time, and were often instrumental in finding benefactors to develop the settlements. There is no doubt that they were looked up to and greatly admired, and when we meet people of our generation who went through these clubs, they speak of them with great reverence and almost a sense of awe.

Unknowingly, we challenged their position and sometimes, it would seem, their ideas and ways of doing things. This was because we came from the same background as the parents of our members. We'd lived in the same streets, gone to the same schools, attended the same synagogue, shopped at the same shops. We continued to mix with them socially and joined in their celebrations and sometimes shared their troubles and sorrows. Even after we married and moved what then seemed a long way away – all of three miles – our life was still centred on our family and friends, on the synagogue, on the club – on Clapton.

Looking back to 1946, Miriam Moses's advice gave us the confidence to go forward. In retrospect, though, it is clear that it was the qualities of the Clapton community and its young people that shaped the Clapton Jewish Youth Centre and made it so vibrant and apparently such a big part of so many people's lives.

APPENDIX

Former members, managers, leaders and parents who have contributed with interviews or questionnaires

Marina (Pincus) Appel

Stanley Appel

Cyril Brill

Ronnie Brown

Steve Chess

Lisa (Eppel) Cohen

Martin Compton

Lorna (Greene) Compton

Roy Collins

Sally (Rose) Davies

Mirelle (Nestel) Dessau

Maurice Garfield

Ralph Goldstaub

Barrie Hyman

Raymond Keene

Jeffrey Leifer

Joan (Freedman) Leifer

Hymie Lipman

Lord Michael Levy

Harold Margolis

Esna (Altwarg) Kaufman

Martin Kaufman

Claire Rayner

Alan Rose

Pam Spector

Norman Spector

Shirley (Fox) Sherman

Rochelle (Jacobs) Snowden

Frances (Bookatz) Seaton

Helen Shapiro

Malcolm Stella

Jean (Hersh) Taylor

Brian Winston

Norma (Yellin) Levenstein

Beverly (Bersh) Zacaria

Parents' Association – Betty Silver

Association for Jewish Youth – Michael Goldstein MBE

Parents' Association
There were so many parents involved in the club, it is not possible to list them all. I am therefore only recording the names of the chairmen, who were as follows:

Emmanuel Lightman

Harry Gnessen

Morris Leifer

Jack Silver